The Masks of Melancholy

Other books by John White

The Cost of Commitment
The Fight: a practical handbook of Christian living
People in Prayer: portraits from the Bible
Eros Defiled: the Christian and sexual guilt
Parents in Pain
The Golden Cow: materialism in the twentieth-century church

THE MASKS OF MELANCHOLY

A Christian psychiatrist
looks at depression and suicide

John White

Inter-Varsity Press

Inter-Varsity Press
38 De Montfort Street, Leicester LE1 7GP, England

Acknowledgement is made for the use of the following copyright material:

"Beck's Inventory for Measuring Depression," pp. 68–69, is taken from Aaron T. Beck, *Depression: Causes and Treatment*, University of Pennsylvania Press, Philadelphia, 1967, and used by permission.

"Zung's Self Rating Depression Scale," p. 70, is taken from W. K. Zung, "From Art to Science, The Diagnosis and Treatment of Depression," *Archives of General Psychiatry* 29 (1973), pp. 328–327, copyright 1973, American Medical Association, and used by permission.

"Hamilton Rating Scale for Depression," pp. 72–73, is taken from M. Hamilton, "A Rating Scale for Depression," *Journal of Neurology, Neurosurgery and Psychiatry* 23 (1960), pp. 56–62, and used by permission.

First published in the United States of America
First British edition 1982
Reprinted 1983, 1985

British Library Cataloguing in Publication Data
White, John
  The masks of melancholy.
  1. Mental illness
  I. Title
  616.89   RC454

ISBN 0-85110-442-8

Printed in Great Britain by Collins, Glasgow

Inter-Varsity Press is the publishing division of the Universities and Colleges Christian Fellowship (formerly the Inter-Varsity Fellowship), a student movement linking Christian Unions in universities and colleges throughout the United Kingdom and the Republic of Ireland, and a member movement of the International Fellowship of Evangelical Students. For information about local and national activities write to UCCF, 38 De Montfort Street, Leicester LE1 7GP.

To those who still travel
in the Valley
of Deepest Darkness

Contents

Preface

Sometimes writers bite off more than they can chew. I may well have done so in writing about depression and suicide. Yet I felt it would be better to try and fail than not to make the attempt at all. I am sure that critics of what I have expressed will not be wanting, which is only as it should be. My hope is that they will make their criticisms in the spirit that I have tried to write in; that is, with no desire to belittle theories I may not entirely agree with, but to make a contribution which will help to alleviate the distress of "those who dwell in darkness."

Because I hope that my book will be read by counselors of various kinds (doctors, ministers, social workers and psychologists) I have included some technical details here and there which may not concern the general reader. Some involve tests for depression. Others deal with theoretical and even neurophysiological concepts. I hope, however, that they will provide a background for those who have special interests and serve as an introduction to more extensive literature.

Part I
Christianity
& Mental
Illness

1
The Differences in Depression

If there is a hell on earth, it is to be found in a melancholy man's heart.
Robert Burton, The Anatomy of Melancholy.

Scenario 1: Silent as Stone

I vividly recall how she stood in one corner of my office, half turned to me, half turned to the wall. A thin, little sixty-year-old lady as still as stone. Silent. Her family said she had scarcely spoken for days and that she had not eaten for weeks. She was dressed in black and gray.

Very gently I encouraged her to speak. Eventually she did, but in a voice so low that I had to strain my ears to catch the words that crept from between her lips.

"I'm going to die. . . . I deserve to die. . . . God is punishing me. . . . We have no money. My husband is bankrupt. . . . He's trying to poison me. . . . They all are. . . ." (Her husband was not bankrupt.)

"But why?"

"Because I'm wicked." She still would not look at me.

"I'd like to help you."

"No, Dr. White. You'd poison me too."

"Surely you know me better than that."

"But I *have* to be poisoned. I'm bad."

"Too bad to be forgiven?"

"God has forsaken me. I'm too wicked."

From that point on she remained silent and remote. She would not eat. She would not drink. Skin hung dryly and loosely from her tiny frame. We could have force-fed her by inserting a nasogastric tube, but she would have pulled it out. We could have given her intravenous fluids, but she would have torn them out too unless we bound her helplessly. And even then I believe she would have died.

Five weeks later, after four electroshock treatments and with the help of medication, she had gradually returned to her usual self—energetic, cheerful, busy and full of talk about "the joy of the Lord." She had regained ten of the thirty pounds she lost during her depressive illness and was full of plans for the future. She ate well, slept well and had all the energy she needed.

Scenario 2: Troubled for Weeks

One of my sons, a twenty-year-old, had been looking listless and troubled for weeks. He was sleeping poorly and seemed to be losing weight. One day he called my office from home.

"I want to talk to you, Dad."

"Sure. When?"

"As soon as you have an hour. No rush."

His voice was flat but I thought I detected an edge to it. "What about tonight?"

"I'd like to see you in your office."

In my office? That was a new one. We set an hour that suited us both.

He looked tense when he arrived and sat stiffly in his chair. He said he didn't know where to begin, but once he got started the words poured in a steady stream.

An hour or so later he was smiling, leaning back relaxed with his legs stretched out in front of him.

"You've no idea how glad I am I came," he said quietly.

That evening my wife commented, "He came back like he was walking on air. I'm so glad, whatever it was, that he talked it out with you."

Scenario 3: "What about Forgiveness?"

He was a forty-year-old bachelor who had already spent several weeks on the psychiatric ward. He believed he had cancer and that we were all lying to him when we told him he showed no evidence of it. He had no energy and no appetite, and he couldn't sleep. He was given antipsychotic pills, mood-elevating pills, and ten electroconvulsive treatments. Result: no change.

I had him in my office to try to get a better handle on what could be wrong. As he talked about earlier years in his life, two things seemed to trouble him. He had drunk a bottle of beer several years before when his doctor had told him not to. More significantly, he had avoided enlisting in World War 2, and felt bad that some of his friends had died in Europe. Curiously he felt equally bad about both his "sins."

As he talked something mysterious happened. An invisible door swung open between us so that our naked spirits faced each other. "What about forgiveness?" I asked him.

"I want it so *bad.*"

"What's your religion?"

"Russian Orthodox."

"And what does your priest say about how you get to be forgiven?"

"He doesn't talk too much. We go to confession."

"And what does that do?"

"I don't often go."

I groped for words. "But if you do go, why would God forgive you?"

"Because Christ died. He shed blood."

"*So?*"

"But I'm too bad for that."

Unaccountably I grew angry. No logical reason. It just happened. "What d'you mean you're too bad?"

His voice was rising like my own. "I don't deserve ever to be forgiven."

"You're darn right you don't!"

He looked up at me surprised. "I can't be a hypocrite. I gotta make amends."

It may be hard to believe, but I found my anger increasing. "And who d'you think you are to say Christ's death was not enough for you? Who are you to feel you must add your miserable pittance to the great gift God offers you? Is his sacrifice not good enough for the likes of you?"

We continued to stare at each other, and suddenly he began both to cry and to pray at once. I wish I could remember his exact words. There's something indescribably refreshing about the first real prayer a man prays, especially when he doesn't know proper prayer-talk. As nearly as I can recall he said something like this: "God, I didn't know. I'm real sorry. I didn't mean to offend you." More sobs, tears, running nose. I passed him a box of Kleenex. "God, thank you. . . . It's amazing. . . . I didn't know it worked like that. . . . I thought . . . but, God, I don't know much. . . . Gee, God, I don't know how to say it. Thank you. Thanks an awful lot. Gee, God, *thank* you."

I prayed, my normal fluency a little hampered by his emotion, while he mopped up his face with Kleenex.

His eyes were shining and he shook my hand. "Thanks, Doc. Thanks a lot. How come nobody ever told me before?" We cut out all the medication.

During the following week I deliberately refrained from doing more than bid him, "Good morning, how are you?" each day. I wanted to let others record his progress. And they did. The notes on his chart read, "Remarkable improvement. No longer seems depressed. Paranoid ideation not expressed. Making realistic plans for future."

Then one day he said, "Doc, I know you're busy, but I just gotta talk to you." As soon as he sat down he started. "I don't know how to say it, Doc, but it's like I've been blind all my life and now—well, now I can see." He had never read a Bible, never sung an evangelical hymn. He didn't know he was quoting.

Carefully I checked his mental status as we talked. No depression. No sign of mania. Paranoid thinking and nihilistic delusions—only the barest trace. He was practically made whole.

Scenario 4: Needing a Workout
Henry Guenther came round to my office just before noon. "Ready for the Y today, John?"

"Oh, I don't know. I'm tired, Henry—listless, can't seem to get anything done. Sort of depressed."

Henry and I used to run round the track for a mile or so and then swim a number of laps each day.

"Come on! You need to get out of this place for a while."

Forty-five minutes later, steamed, shampooed and showered, I rubbed my tingling skin with the abundance of white towels the YMCA supplies for its health-club members. Then I sat to relax a moment or two in front of my locker, before the luxury of getting dressed slowly. I was a new man. Mentally I thanked God for Henry who doggedly would drag me to the Y each lunch time.

Defying Definition
I have several reasons for sketching these four scenarios. Each picture has to do with depression, but clearly not all the "depressions" are the same in quantity nor even in quality. My morning blues in my office were not to be compared with

the torture oppressing the lady who stood in the corner of that same office some weeks before. My *mood* was depressed, but I was not "sick" in any sense. A good physical workout and the easy camaraderie of the health club cleared it away as the sun clears morning mists. Neither my son, nor the lady I first mentioned, nor even the man who found forgiveness, would have been uplifted by sweating and puffing around the track or by feeling the needling of a high-pressure shower massaging their muscles. Whether a mere mood, a malady, a madness or a spiritual bondage, each of our four conditions could be called depression. Yet each differed from the others. Therefore, at some point we are going to have to attempt to define the word *depression*. For the moment, however, we will let it pass.

As early as 1917 Sigmund Freud wrote, "Even in descriptive psychiatry the definition of melancholia is uncertain; it takes on various clinical forms (some of them suggesting somatic rather than psychogenic affections) that do not seem definitely to warrant reduction to a unit."[1] It is a pity many of his psychoanalytic followers fail to pay heed to his words.

I don't want to begin by dodging an ideological battle, but I cannot stress the differences too much. Counselors who try to help depressed people, and authors who write books about the subject, generally oversimplify the issue. Depression has many faces. It cannot be relieved on the basis of one simple formula, arising as it does by numerous and complex mechanisms, and plummeting sometimes to depths where its victims are beyond the reach of verbal communication. There are mysteries about it which remain unsolved. No one theoretical framework is adequate to describe it.

I hesitate to write about it because many of my professional colleagues hold rigidly to exclusive, often dogmatic and contradictory theories about it. Psychiatrists, psychologists, social workers, spiritual counselors and a host of other would-be helpers despise one another's viewpoints. They cannot communicate nor do they seem to wish to. Each school has its own technical terms and its own model so that intelligent discussion is hampered both by needless indignation and by semantic confusion. The very language we use is different so that by creating new realities with new words, other "realities" are meaningless to us.

I would like to evade controversy altogether, proceeding directly to descriptions of what I call the many masks of melancholy, and to suggest methods of restoring its victims. But I must be honest about my presuppositions and my philosophical and scientific reasoning.

I shall have to discuss the question of whether depression or some varieties of it constitute illness in any sense, or whether they are better regarded as forms of behavior or even of communication. And if the question of illness arises, we shall have to face the question: Illness of what? Of body? Of mind? Of spirit? If it is an illness of mind, we must ask, What is mind? These are the issues found in chapters two and three.

Part two goes on to discuss how psychologists and psychiatrists have analyzed the symptoms and the depth of various depressions. Part three considers ten different models theorists have used to understand depression and concludes by looking at suicide.

For some readers portions of part three will be technical. But if you have had professional training, or have already been indoctrinated by some book or course, let me plead that you suspend judgment until you have opened yourself to more broadly based thinking. Narrow bigotry, whether in the human sciences or in philosophy, tends only to bolster our inflated egos and to lessen the chances for wholeness of those we seek to help.

The fact is that no single theory, however carefully applied, alleviates every depression. Yet instead of admitting that our theory may not always be appropriate we blame the depressed person. He is "uncooperative," "lacks motivation" or is "incapable of insight." She may be labeled "immature" or "manipulative," or be accused of "playing games." Sometimes we apply such labels accurately. At other times we see people through the spectacles of our theoretical prejudice. It is easier to blame the client and keep our theory intact.

Pastors and religious counselors have their own ways of doing the same thing. The words they use may be different, but they are words that cast the blame on the depressed person, who is described as "lacking in faith," "full of self-pity," "unwilling to rejoice in the Lord," "giving place to the devil" or "needing a kick in the pants." Sometimes the pastor is right. But there are other times when the real problem lies in the pastor's inadequate understanding.

Fortunately the late seventies were characterized by attempts to build bridges between the principal theories. Leading thinkers from different schools, with a new humility and a new curiosity, have been acknowledging not only that their points of view are only partially true but also that other models have merits too. The last section of this book, part four, considers how the various models have been applied.

We often remind physicians that the patient is more important than the theory, and surgeons that the operation is *not* successful if the patient dies. I, too, have my biases and must be open to correction. But my main concern is for depressed people. Let us beware lest they become the victims of our incompetence and conceit.

I grow saddened and sometimes bitter when I think of people who suffer needlessly when help is at hand. I cannot blame those whose pride and bigotry create needless suffering in depressed people. I too have been bigoted and proud. Still less can my rage serve any use when I think of the millions who do not even seek help. So I have chosen to channel bitterness into the kind of book which I hope may result in better communication among professionals and more effective relief for some of the sufferers.

2
Sin, Disease
& the Devil

*The mentally ill have always been
with us–to be feared, marvelled at,
laughed at, pitied or tortured but
all too seldom cured. Their existence shakes us to the core of our
being, for they make us painfully*
*aware that sanity is a fragile thing.
To cope with their ills man has
always needed a science that could
penetrate to where the natural
sciences cannot–into the universe
of man's mind.   F. G. Alexander*

If we are to have a Christian understanding of depression and
particularly of the more serious forms of depression, we must
first seek answers to certain questions. What is physical disease, and how (if at all) is it related to sin? Is mental disease
related to sin and, if so, is it related to sin in the same way as
physical disease, or in different ways? What is the nature of
mental illness, and how (if at all) does it differ from physical
illness? Can demons make us ill, physically or mentally? If so
how can we distinguish demonic states from mental and physical illness of other kinds? How do we define mind?

Physical Disease and Sin
There are indeed connections between sin and sickness. Sin
gives rise to disease in two ways: directly and indirectly. All

diseases arise indirectly from sin while some in addition may represent the direct results from sin. Sin produced humanity's Fall. With the Fall came human mortality, making our bodies subject to death processes which impair our function and eventually kill us. God had warned (" . . . in the day that you eat of it you shall die," Gen 2:17). But the warning was in vain. When tempted, first the woman, then the man fell into disobedience.

"To the woman he [God] said, 'I will greatly multiply your pain in childbearing; in pain you shall bring forth children' " (Gen 3:16). Pain began with disobedience in Eden.

The curse was not confined to the human race but blighted all creation, of which we are an integral part. Having initially pronounced a blessing over creation, God now cursed it. "Cursed is the ground because of you; in toil you shall eat of it all the days of your life; thorns and thistles it shall bring forth to you" (Gen 3:17-18).

Childbearing had evidently not been planned as a painful process. The ground was not originally designed to produce thorns and thistles. But conditions changed. Humanity and humanity's environment both deteriorated and became other than God had purposed.

And the most striking element in the curse was the sentence of death. "In the sweat of your face you shall eat bread till you return to the ground, for out of it you were taken; you are dust, and to dust you shall return" (Gen 3:19).

So death became king of the human species, and human beings became mortal, subject to decay, disease and their new sovereign. The seed of human beings, like seeds of plants and animals, carried with it the touch of death. New and distorted forms arose as the environment changed, and while there may be singular beauty in some of them, it is beauty reflected in a distorted mirror. From that time to this, diseases have ravaged human communities. No disease-free society has ever existed. Modern medicine may have accomplished minor miracles, but our deteriorating relationship with the environment threatens us with new and uglier forms of disease.

We can say then that all sickness arises indirectly from sin in the sense that sin has blighted our race as a whole, rendering us all subject to degeneration, to decay and to invasion by hostile organisms. What we must not always say is that Aunt Mary's rheumatism is a sign that Aunt Mary did something wicked or that God is punishing her with painful joints.

A direct relationship may or may not exist. Today I spent time with a man whose brain was so severely damaged by drinking and by neglect of a proper diet that he seems to have permanent difficulty in maintaining his balance, has problems with his vision and such a gross impairment of his memory that he cannot remember where he is sixty seconds after he has been told. His liver may eventually pack up. If perpetual drunkenness is sinful, then my patient's sickness arises from his sin. Likewise, if sexual promiscuity is sinful (and Scripture says it is), then the ravages of venereal disease which sometimes accompany promiscuity are the direct results of sin.

But there are less obvious ways in which personal sin can cause sickness. The apostle James seems to hint at them (Jas 5:13-16), and many Christians report instances where confession of sin has led to healing. Kurt Koch, for instance, writes of a farmer's dying wife who pleaded for an evangelical Christian to visit her that she might unburden herself before she died. During the visit for "a period lasting two hours, the woman made an open confession of her sins. She was now prepared to die. However events proved otherwise. Later when the Christian brother visited the farm again, he found the farmer's wife standing in the yard with a look of joy on her face. He could hardly believe his eyes. What had happened? It transpired that after she had confessed her sins, in addition to forgiving her, the Lord had also touched her body and healed her. Yet at the time of her confession the thought of healing had never entered her mind."[1]

Mental Illness and Sin

We may say then that all sickness is a consequence of sin in the sense that it results from humanity's Fall and mortality, and that in addition there are times when sickness results from specific personal sins. But what are we to say of so-called mental illness? Is it true that because we are fallen human beings we are exposed to insanity too? Or might mental illness be at times due to specific sins committed by the sufferer?

The questions are not easy ones. Mental illness has to do with *mind*. And mind is thought of as a nonmaterial entity, somehow related to brain. Later we shall look at the relationship between body and mind more closely. For the present we will content ourselves with noting at least one biblical account of insanity which arose because of specific personal sin—the sin of pride.

Warned by the prophet Daniel that he must repent and renounce his sins if insanity were not to overtake him, Nebuchadnezzar, Babylonian ruler of an empire, continued to satisfy his insatiable ego with fantasies of personal glory and power. A year later he was smitten (in midfantasy, so to speak) with madness. For seven years he lived like a wild animal outside the pale of civilization. But at the end of that period Nebuchadnezzar tells us, "I . . . lifted my eyes to heaven, and my reason returned to me, and I blessed the Most High, and praised and honored him who lives for ever" (Dan 4:34).

Inferences based on one passage must be tentative. Many guesses have been made as to the nature of Nebuchadnezzar's condition, which I hesitate to diagnose, but it is clear that he suffered some form of mental illness. I must also be clear that his condition did not arise from demonic possession or oppression. I say this because Daniel seemed to accept Nebuchadnezzar's own account of what happened without comment. Daniel was trained in Chaldean lore, with its ideas of magic, divination and demons. He was also familiar with the powers of darkness and with the nature of battle in the heavenlies through his extraordinary prayer life (Dan 10:10-14). Had demons been responsible for Nebuchadnezzar's insanity, it would be remarkable that Daniel should record its description (in detail, together with Nebuchadnezzar's interpretation that he lost and subsequently regained his "reason") and not mention demons.

One further inference may be made from Nebuchadnezzar's story. His mental illness represented divine chastisement for his personal sins. His restoration followed the lifting up of his eyes to heaven (Dan 4:34). It would seem possible then that a wrong relation with God exposes us to the risk of insanity, and that a right relation with God is a move in the direction of mental health. And if, after all, God designed us to be related to him, what would be more natural? It would be unwise, however, to be more specific. Some people remain sane in spite of a wrong relationship with God, and others become insane in spite of a good relationship with him.

The Genesis story of the Fall can also be interpreted to imply that poor mental health is something we are all exposed to. Disobedience in Eden led to fear, to the shame of nakedness (Gen 3:10) and to a change in sexual relationships (Gen 3:16), three things related to mental health. My personal conviction is that our general vulnerability to poor mental health began at the dawn of human history and must not be seen as arising always as a consequence of personal sin or of demonic power. Mental health is like physical health. We are all vulnerable to its loss. And in addition sometimes it may arise because of specific, personal sin.

But there is a further point we must discuss as we look at mental health in the ancient world. Experts in the human sciences arrogantly declare (presumably without having researched ancient literature) that the ancients in their ignorance always saw mental illness as something demonic. This is untrue.

Already we have noted the case of Nebuchadnezzar. We might also look at King David. In danger of his life in the city-kingdom of Gath, he pretended to be insane. "He changed his behavior before them, and feigned himself mad in their hands, and made marks on the doors of the gate, and let his spittle run down his beard. Then said [King] Achish to his servants, 'Lo, you see the man is mad; why then have you brought him to me? Do I lack madmen, that you have brought this fellow to play the madman in my presence?' " (1 Sam 21:13-15).

You will notice two things. David had a concept of madness, a concept which was shared by Achish, King of Gath. Both knew what madness looked like. Yet David was also aware of the demonic, and evidently distinguished it from madness. Plagued by an "evil spirit from the Lord," his master Saul made several attempts to murder David (1 Sam 16:14-23; 19:8-10). David knew from terrifying firsthand experience the power of demonic influence. It was not demonic affliction that he mimicked in Gath but madness. Therefore, at that period there must have been a general understanding that both kinds of conditions existed and that they were distinguishable. Several other references to madness make us aware that the concept was common to ancient Hebrew culture (Deut 28:28; Eccles 1:17; 2:2, 12; 7:25; 9:3; 10:13; Jer 25:16; 50:38; 51:7; Zech 12:4).

In the New Testament there is madness too. Festus accused Paul in a phrase which roughly corresponds to "driven round the bend." One of the words he used is a word from which we derive our word *manic* (Acts 26:24). Jesus was accused both of being "manic" and of being demonized. On the other hand when Rhoda announced to a startled group of disciples that Peter was standing at the door, they promptly accused her of being mad or "manic." Now the word *manic* does not mean "demonized." However crazy Rhoda might have seemed, her brothers and sisters would hardly have accused her of *that* (Acts 12:15).

Again, Paul warned the church of Antioch that the way in which they had been exercising the gift of tongues might lead an unconverted person to regard them as crazy (1 Cor 14:23). Two other words in the New Testament constitute roots from which we derive the modern terms *paranoia* and *schizophrenia* (see Lk 6:11 and 2 Pet 2:16).

Demons and Mental Illness

Certainly in New Testament times there were demons aplenty. Jesus cast them out. His disciples cast them out. More to the point Jesus predicted that a sign of true discipleship following his ascension would be the casting out of demons. "And these signs," he said, "will accompany those who believe: in my name they will cast out demons . . ." (Mk 16:17). Unusual mental states in the New Testament as well as the Old were seen to result from madness as well as from demons, and the two states could be distinguished.

Among modern Christians I find a wide range of attitudes about demons. There are enthusiasts who seem overeager both to spot demons and to bind them, exorcise them or consign them to the outer darkness where they belong. Some enthusiasts claim a special "ministry" in the occult. At the other extreme are Christians who do not believe in demons at all. Between the two extremes are those of us who are far less certain of ourselves. We believe demons exist. We believe they are still around. Yet in spite of our biblical and theological studies and our psychological sophistication, we are better at talking about demons than at spotting them or dealing with them. We are, as it were, neither fish nor fowl in the matter of demonology.

Let me make a couple of preliminary observations. First, I have no question that demons are alive and well in the West today. Second, there are dangers in all three positions I outlined above. "For we are not contending against flesh and blood," Paul writes to Christians who would strive to live for Christ, "but against the principalities, against the powers, against the world rulers of this present darkness, against the spiritual hosts of wickedness in the heavenly places" (Eph 6:12). The foul hordes are about us. We ignore them at our peril. They will oppose the slightest attempt we make to follow Christ. Those who profess not to believe in them or who ridicule any concern about demons today will never prove effective soldiers of Christ. Evil is personal, potent, real and rampant.

But some enthusiasts are exposed to danger, the danger of being mocked as fools by the very enemy they talk so much about, as well as of doing more harm than good. They seek to cast out demons where sometimes no demons exist. They may unwittingly pander to the weak consciences of some who want an excuse (an obliging demon) for what amounts to personal sin that needs to be confessed and put aside. Again, enthusiasts may pay more attention to Satan than to Christ and may be more occupied with his power than with the glory of Jesus. Or they may add greatly to the distress of Christians by calling on them to renounce and resist nonexistent demons. Some suffering souls are already the victims of debilitating sickness and now have foisted on them by their spiritual counselors an additional burden of false guilt, false guilt about not resisting the dark powers enough.

Yet the middle-of-the-road position also has its dangers. We say we believe, but do we? To profess to believe that imminent peril exists but that we are unable either to see or to deal with the peril is a sorry position to be in. Are we perhaps respectable fence-straddlers? We cannot be accused of not taking Scripture seriously, for we say we believe. But our so-called belief would be impotent before the man possessed of many demons who tore the chains out of rock. Perhaps we should be more willing to run the risk of being fools or of getting our hands dirty.

For the present, however, a question remains. How do demons relate to mental illness today? We say that in Scripture both entities seemed to exist and to be distinguished. If we broaden the question and ask, "How does sickness in general relate to demon activity?" we will begin to see an answer. In Mark 9:14-29 we are given a vivid description of a deaf-mute boy who had epileptiform seizures and who was cured when Jesus cast out a tormenting demon. Now deafness and epilepsy are commonly regarded as physical illnesses. Yet in this instance they had a demonic cause. On another occasion Jesus expelled an evil spirit from a deaf and blind man (Mt 12:22-24) to cure these "physical" conditions. Yet on other occasions he cured deafness, dumbness, blindness and other sickness without casting out demons, treating them as physical infirmities, related neither to personal sin nor to demons (see Jn 9:1-7).

If for a moment we can cling to the term *mental illness,* and not be overeager to exaggerate the differences between mental illness and physical illness, we will at least see the possibility that the Old Testament and New are consistent in seeing all sickness (mental or physical) as arising either from demonic activity or from human mortality, and calling either for exorcism or for cure, according to their nature. Such is the opinion of a number of well-known Christian psychiatrists and psychologists. Dr. Alfred Lechler, an associate of Kurt Koch, assumes the distinction between demonic and other mental conditions when he writes, "One can . . . understand why a number of mistakes are made in diagnosis, especially since many Christian workers are prone to label any mental illness as an expression of the demonic, and since many psychiatrists regard possession as a type of mental illness."[2] Interestingly enough he goes on to make the statement, "It is almost invariably true . . . that if a person is forever talking about being possessed, he is really suffering from some form of mental illness rather than from demonic influence."[3] Indeed the problem is compounded by the fact that in much insanity, hallucinations and delusions are woven out of the raw material in our memories. If our thoughts include the demonic, then we will hear "demonic" voices when we become crazy or have delusions about demons in and around us. We weave insanity out of threads of thought already in our minds.

Several recent discussions touch on the distinction between demonic and psychiatric conditions,[4] but I will limit my discussion to what I have experienced.

Demonic Insanity

Earlier I mentioned my difficulties in the matter of demon possession or, to use the New Testament word, *demonization*. I believe that certain (possibly many) persons diagnosed as suffering from mental disease are in fact demonized. Yet I confess that I cannot shed my Western mindset without a tremendous struggle which makes it hard for me to be sure whether demons are present on a given occasion. I also confess that I lack faith when faced with my right to invoke the authority of Jesus and that my pride makes me fearful of looking like a fool in front of my colleagues and students. I make my confessions with shame, though I also want to make it clear that I wait on God, frequently requesting the discernment and authority that I lack.

A number of things puzzle me. I am humbled to observe that sometimes brand new Christians are used by God to cast out demons that I have failed to cast out. I am also puzzled that I myself have been used to cast them out, only to realize in retrospect that this is what has happened. I am also bewildered that self-proclaimed exorcists who are to my mind complete fools and sometimes knaves are occasionally able to cast out demons by means of the weirdest rituals. Finally, I am uncertain about my right to remove demons from those patients of mine who seem to be possessed by them and who refuse to give me their consent to deal with the real problem.

For those interested in the subject I would recommend a book edited by John Warwick Montgomery, *Demon Possession,* published by Bethany Press. It reflects the thinking of sociologists, anthropologists, psychologists, psychiatrists, biblical scholars and theologians in papers read at a symposium sponsored by the Christian Medical Society a few years ago. I contributed two papers to it, but recommend the book because of the bibliographies that it contains and because of the wide variety of information.

Let me in addition describe as accurately as I can some of the cases I have encountered. My first was in a missionary training camp. Late at night I was awakened with a request to see a forty-year-old bachelor, a missionary candidate who was behaving strangely. I begged to be left alone with him, mainly because I did not wish my doubts and uncertainties to be witnessed by the other missionary candidates.

The man in question was sitting upright in bed, slowly and systematically plucking handfuls of hair from his head. A pile of hair lay on his lap. He would have been judged psychotic by any psychiatrist. Initially he seemed unaware of my presence and neither looked at me nor responded to my questions.

My patient seemed profoundly depressed. I found myself urging him to forsake his sin, even though I did not know of any sin of which he might have been guilty. My words, however, penetrated his armor. Slowly he began to respond, lashing out at me with accusations about my own sins and failures. He addressed himself to the foot of his bed rather than to me, carefully avoiding my gaze as he slowly worked himself up to a frenzied verbal attack on me, an attack totally inconsistent with his usually courteous and gentle personality. In the end he agreed to let me pray with him. Following the prayer he lay back in bed and fell asleep. In the morning he had no recollection of what had occurred. He was alert and restored to his rightful mind. Subsequently he married, had children, served God faithfully for many years on the mission field, and to the best of my knowledge never had any similar trouble again. My personal belief is that his fugue state (a condition in which someone is either mute or unresponsive) was demonic in origin and that unwittingly I had been the means of dealing with it.

Another case (also described in the book *Demon Possession*) concerned a young Lutheran deaconess who was the organizing secretary of one of the three gay leagues in Winnipeg. Following a suicide attempt, she was admitted to the hospital where at the time I practiced. Her behavior suggested that she suffered from a bipolar depression (a type of illness in which there is mixture of both manic and depressive features), and I tried to treat her accordingly. The medication I gave her seemed to settle her.

I invited her to a Bible study in my home. When it was over she asked me, "What does it mean when you try to sing, 'Oh, how I love Jesus' and yet what comes out is, 'Oh, how I *hate* Jesus'?" I asked her whether she was questioning me about demons, and she admitted that she was. She also commented that in Lutheran services she consistently turned liturgy and hymns into blasphemous utterances, utterances she was only aware of in retrospect. Her pastor confirmed this.

She described a previous experience of a "friendly ghost" who frequently visited an apartment she once shared with another woman. "We never saw him, but we often heard him crossing the living room as the floorboards creaked. It was fun." Soon, however, she was robbed of her rest by weird knockings, tappings and creakings, and left the apartment for somewhere more tranquil.

I agreed to attempt to deal with the problem of demons next time she came to the office. At that point she was attending our day-care program. When she came I addressed myself to the demon or demons, commanding him or them to leave her. She seemed to go into a trance in which she alternately laughed insanely and wept horrendously. I had a peculiar subjective sense that I was being threatened and that my wife and children would be attacked. After an hour or so I said, "Well, I guess time's up." As I said this, there was a final despairing laugh, and my patient came out of her trance.

Her first words (if I remember correctly) were "My God! What have you been doing to me? I feel like I've been dragged through a hedge backwards!" She showed me the palms of her hands, where she had pierced them with her fingernails in the intensity of the session. I noticed as she remained seated that the lap of her tweed skirt was soaked with her tears in a circular area about six or seven inches in diameter.

During the subsequent hour or so three different members of the day-care nursing staff knocked on my door, all with the same question and comment, "What have you done to that girl? She's completely different." Yet I felt the work was not finished.

Several days later she visited a charismatic group and begged their help. A new convert, a young teen-aged girl, said, "Demon whose name is Legion, come out of her!" At that point several things happened. My patient fell to the ground and the whole group was stricken with terror. Almost immediately, however, what they described as a "baptism of love" fell on them, and they kneeled or stood round her, assuring her of God's love for her. She herself recollects hearing someone saying over and over again, "He couldn't possibly love me," and slowly realizing that the voice was her own.

On her next visit to me she was radiant with joy. "Know what?" she said, "I'm no longer a lesbian."

"Oh," I responded, "what made you decide to quit?"

"Decide nothing!" she cried, "When the demons were gone, I just wasn't!"

Let me make a couple of comments. The first is that we

would be foolish to conclude that all gays are demon possessed and need to be exorcised. The other is that my patient not only was no longer gay but that she subsequently "went straight" for many years and became an outstanding Christian witness. I have not been in contact with her for a couple of years, but there is no question in my mind that the work God did in her life represented true deliverance, no matter how God accomplished it.

Another young woman who consulted me did so because of her rage toward her second child. She seemed normal apart from depression. She reproached herself bitterly. Because she might have injured the baby, I suggested she take it to the X-ray department. The X rays showed a skull fracture and fractures of the long bones. Clearly the baby should be taken temporarily out of danger and into custody. Arrangements were made with a foster mother, the real mother seeing and feeding the child daily in the foster mother's presence.

My patient had been an adopted child who had been battered by her Christian adoptive parents. She had experienced little normal love. A few months before coming to see me, she had been seized by a strange compulsion to put out the light in a room where the baby was sleeping, feeling that she must do so by seizing the light bulb with her bare hands. Only when her hands were badly burned did she release the bulb. Local Christians felt she was under the influence of demons and tried unsuccessfully to exorcise her. I thought that she had been psychotic, and I tried to treat her depression while seeing her with her husband in an attempt to help their troubled marriage.

In the months that followed several more attempts were made to exorcise her by different charismatic leaders as they visited the city. None of them was able to alleviate her distress. Meanwhile I began slowly to conclude that her anxiety and depression were not of the kind that would respond either to medication or to normal counseling. To the best of my memory I made no attempt to exorcise her.

While the baby was still in custody, my patient and her husband spent a week at a Christian camp where one of the speakers again sought to rid her of demons. He proceeded to name them, to command them to leave her and to call on her to renounce them one by one.

She came back to Winnipeg totally changed. The agitated, overly dependent personality had given place to a relaxed and gentle wife and mother. So profound was the change that the agnostic social worker who supervised the visits to the foster mother called me by telephone to suggest that the baby could safely be returned to her. Like me, she was astonished at the depth and reality of the change. The baby was restored to her and my patient had no further difficulty with her rages.

I am now convinced that her condition was demonic and that the last exorcist must have had something that the others lacked. At my request my patient gave me a tape containing her exorcist's teachings about demonism. But if I had hoped to learn anything, I was quickly disillusioned. Arrogant, pompous nonsense would best describe the tape's contents. To this day I shake my head in bewilderment. I can only conclude that ability to cast out demons is not the exclusive prerogative of godly and intelligent people.

One day a Christian girl in her early twenties came to consult me about her problems. She was depressed, had made one or two suicide attempts, smoked marijuana and was living common-law with a man she did not care for. What most troubled her was her recently acquired gift of clairvoyance. She had no idea from where or how the gift had come to her, except that on entering certain older homes in the city she could see into the past. The house would come alive with persons wearing the kind of dress common about a hundred years ago. She could observe them and listen to their trivial conversations. She did not particularly enjoy her gift. I examined her as carefully as I could and found no psychiatric disability apart from her depressed mood. As I continued to question her, she described her attempts a year or two earlier to "project" her spirit in search of a dead friend.

Her Mennonite parents had forbidden her to see the man she hoped to marry. A week after the breakup he committed suicide. As she lay in bed at night, she tried in her grief to concentrate on him in a kind of psychic search. After a month or two her attempts were rewarded by dreamlike visits from her dead lover.

I pointed out that she had been fooling around with the occult and could only be helped if she were to confess and forsake her sin. No sooner had I spoken than she got up, a frightened expression on her face and bolted from my office. Once or twice she made distressed telephone calls to me, but as soon as I suggested that she come to see me, she would hang up.

Currently I have more than one husband consulting me, obsessed with feelings of jealousy concerning their wives. The general pattern seems to be that both spouses in each case had indulged in premarital sexual relationships. For a while the marriages had gone well but after some years the husbands grew increasingly apprehensive and depressed as they became the helpless victims of outbursts of rage toward their wives, hurling derision at them for their premarital relations.

The men clearly recognized the injustice of what they were doing yet were helpless in the face of it. Two men suggested to me that their condition might be demonic, without attempting to excuse their behavior. I prayed with each of them and commanded any demonic beings to depart and be gone in the name of Jesus. In the case of the first man, the procedure proved ineffective. The second man on his next visit said, "When I left your office and was walking to the car, I suddenly realized that I was free. The burden had gone completely.

It felt as though a heavy load had been lifted." After a time he decided to test his new freedom in two ways. He accepted an invitation to join a committee on which his wife's former lover also sat. The second thing he did was to attend a social event with his wife. He knew that his wife's former lover would also be present. "But my new-found freedom did not stand the strain. I began to experience inner rage and anxiety," he told me.

There could be any number of explanations to the second man's reaction. Our prayer and my attempted exorcism could have had a placebo effect, the response of a highly suggestible patient. I chose not to adopt that particular idea but to assume that an enemy had truly been cast out and had returned, perhaps with allies, to a house newly swept and garnished. So we embarked on a discussion of the nature of grace and the importance of a personal relationship with Christ. We will carry on our discussion when he next comes to see me. In the meantime I remain with many unanswered questions, and my patient with his jealousy.

Two more incidents occur to me. I remember a shaman who came into the detoxification center I was helping to run some years ago. He was a man in his late fifties. The son and the grandson of shamans, he had been dabbling with the occult for years and shared with me his chief concern, his inability to achieve sexual satisfaction. "I've had it with women, I've had it with boys and I've had it with dogs and other beasts," he told me. "But recently I've been having it with demons, and I can't even have it with boys anymore. Only demons can give it to me, and now they've abandoned me."

He went on to tell me that his hobby was to carve phallic symbols (in the shape of an erect male penis) before which he would place a picture of Jesus, so that he could get Jesus to kiss the phallic symbol.

"You know what you're playing with, don't you?" I asked. "You must get rid of your phallic symbols."

"Yes, but I could always carve more."

"You must still get rid of them. You don't have to carve any more."

He stared at me for a while. Then he said, "I've never before met anyone like you. You have the power of God in you, and I know you really could deal with spirits."

Moments after our conversation, an old (male) flame visited him and urged him to leave the center with him. They left together, and I have never seen them since.

The second incident concerns an East Indian whom some psychiatrists would diagnose as schizo affective (an illness in which a mood disorder and schizophrenialike symptoms are strangely blended). Together with a psychiatric resident, two fourth-year medical students and a couple of nurses, I interviewed him a day or two after his admission. He had been picked up by the police for making obscene phone calls and brought to the hospital because the police judged him to be crazy.

Two themes dominated his thinking. One concerned his ability to project his astral body to distant planets and his determination to commit suicide so that he could be freed altogether from bodily restraints. The second theme had to do with the obscene phone calls. "The spirits make me do it."

"What spirits?" I asked.

"There are three of them. They talk to me. They are kind and keep me from being lonely at night when I have no woman."

"How long have they been with you?"

"It started when I was a child. My father took me to see some holy men. They placed an amulet round my neck and ever since that time. . . ."

"I can get rid of them for you," I said.

An uneasy expression crossed his face, and he drew back from the table. "No. No. I don't want you to do that."

"Yet you know they will eventually destroy you."

"They are kind to me. They take away my loneliness," he reiterated.

There was a pause. Everyone in the room sensed instinctively that we were dealing with more than a psychotic East Indian male. My patient began all over again. "I know you can do it, but I don't want you to. You have the power of God in you. I can feel it. But you must not take away my spirits." So saying he left the room.

As we discussed the incident around the table the most experienced of the nurses (not to my knowledge a Christian) said, "You mustn't take something away from him unless you can give him something to replace it."

She was right. Immediately I followed my patient to tell him of God's concern for him and of the mercy of a loving Christ who could impart all the consolation he needed. He thanked me with tears in his eyes but still shook his head. Two days later he left the hospital against medical advice.

All of these incidents created for me more problems than solutions, but of a number of things I am convinced. First, in no way do they of themselves prove it, yet I believe demonization is a reality. Second, there appears to be many ways to conduct exorcism with the power to do so possessed by people who do not share my personal convictions. Finally, some cases are more "difficult" and demand more prayer and fasting. I both fast and pray (though evidently not enough), but I still grope for a clearer understanding of the events I have described.

3
Healing
& the Mind

If soul and body are said to be incomplete because they cannot exist by themselves. . . I confess that it seems to me to be a con-

tradition for them to be substances. . . . and I know that thinking substance is a complete thing . . . .
In a letter from Descartes to Arnauld

I believe divine healing is real. I believe gifts of healing are still practiced today. Yet I also believe that God in his sovereign purposes does not always grant healing and has never promised always to do so. To assert that all healing is "in the atonement" and therefore for us now, represents both shaky biblical exegesis and poor theology.

Christ did indeed undo all the consequences of sin. His atonement was full, final and complete. Some of its benefits (justification, regeneration and sanctification, for example) are already ours. Others (including immortality and perfect disease-immunity) await us in our resurrection bodies. Glimpses of future glory, in the form of physical healing, may be granted frequently. But the full reward is for a time to come.

Our Greek Heritage

The question of the nature of mental illness and its cure is more difficult than asserting all healing is in the atonement. But to answer this question we must first have a firm hold on the biblical view of human nature. We may assert that we already have such a view. Yet most of us possess a muddled mixture of Greek and Hebrew thought which we have inherited in part through Plato, Aristotle, the Gnostics, St. Thomas Aquinas and the philosopher Descartes. We have divided the human being up into a less important physical part (body and brain) and a more important immaterial part (mind and soul). We have made the matter yet more complicated by discussing the "tripartite man" allegedly found in Scripture and neatly sectioned into three: body, soul and spirit. Please understand that I am not denying that terms such as *soul* and *spirit* are found in Scripture. They are indeed. So are such terms as *mind, heart, will.* The question to be resolved is, What is the relationship among them all?

It would take too long to examine the way each term is used throughout Scripture. But we can look at one or two facts. First, the terms mentioned, if we examine them in their contexts, have a certain amount of overlap. While they are not entirely interchangeable, they are sometimes interchangeable. Second, Scripture seems to conceive of a human being as a whole and not as a creature of divisible parts. We are not meant to have body and mind split up any more than soul and spirit. The doctrine of bodily resurrection should make it clear that we are and always will be bodily creatures.

What we have inherited from the Greeks is a wrong way of perceiving the relationship between mind and body, exalting the one and playing down the other. For in doing so we have fallen into the trap of comparing things that cannot be compared. We are guilty of what some modern philosophers would call a category error, a mixing of apples and oranges.

To compare mind with body is like comparing music with the pianist's fingers. "What matters is the *music!*" we cry. Of course. But no fingers, no music. Clumsy fingers, bad music. Weak fingers, feeble music.

We are groping, perhaps with ideas beyond our grasp. Let me attempt another analogy. We talk about "mind over matter." If we mean by the expression that we should not always give in to our physical weaknesses and cravings, the saying is a good one. But if we mean that there is a sort of wraithlike part of us, the *real* us, called mind that controls the solid part of us called body, we are liable to be confused.

Descartes in his sixth meditation sought to clarify the issue. The self, he decided, was lodged in the body as a pilot in a ship but was more important than a mere pilot. "I am not only lodged in my body as a pilot in a vessel but . . . am very closely united to it, and, so to speak, so intermingled with it that I seem to compose with it one whole. For if this were not the case, when my body is hurt, I, who am merely a thinking being, would not feel pain, for I should perceive this wound by the understanding only, just as the sailor perceives by sight when something is damaged in his vessel."[1] Ultimately, however, the mind was distinct from the body. This view which Descartes expounded gave rise to the term *Cartesian dualism*.

Descartes is aware of his dilemma. If mind is other than body, it must have some very intimate connection with it. But how to describe the connection? He resorts in the end to anatomy. "In examining the matter with care, it seems as though I have clearly ascertained that the part of the body in which the soul [a term Descartes used synonymously with *self* and *mind*] exercises its function immediately is in no way the heart, nor the whole of the brain, but merely the most inward of all its parts, to wit, a very small gland which is situated in the middle of its substance and which is so suspended above the duct whereby the animal spirits in its interior cavities have communications with those in the posterior."[2] The mind, in a word, is found inside a gland, a gland in the brain, a gland which influences parts of the brain and body by *animal spirits,* "material bodies of extreme minuteness" moving very quickly "like particles of flame."[3]

I cannot do justice to Descartes' struggle to understand the nature of the human psyche. But clearly he struggled as we all struggle, to comprehend things immaterial. Our souls do not in fact reside in the pineal bodies inside our skulls. Our minds do not flit from point to point inside our brains and bodies. The attempt to compare mind and body is doomed to failure from the start because of the category error I referred to earlier. One can only compare a thing with something else in the same category. You cannot easily discuss how the color purple is related to a pound of cheddar cheese nor how the sound of middle C relates to the amount of money you have in your bank account.

The Orchestra and the Music

The nearest we can get to describing the relation between mind and body is to consider matter in relation to function. A car runs. A machine works. An orchestra plays music. The relation of mind to body can be compared with the relation between the working of a machine to the machine itself or the relation of the music to the orchestra.

What do psychiatrists think of when they talk about mind? Usually they think of a bunch of bodily functions. I remember. I am conscious. I am aware that I am *me* as distinct from *you.* I feel emotions—anger, sadness, joy. I think, that is to say, I reason. I make decisions. Because these things I do (that is, being conscious, being aware of my identity, remembering, feeling, reasoning, deciding) seem to hang together, I include them under the term *mind.*

But notice. Mind is a group of functions, a group of bodily functions, functions not merely of my brain but of my body as a whole. Take my emotions, for example. As I step off the

43

curb into the path of a car, I hear the screech of brakes, an angry hooting of a horn. I jump back. A car window rolls down and a man screams obscenities at me. How do I feel? Scared. Angry. But what do these feelings consist of? My heart is going *bump, bump, bump* in my chest. My face has turned white. My palms are wet and my fingers are shaking. I feel a little dizzy. All these things—beating heart, white face, sweaty palms, trembling fingers—are bodily sensations, sensations arising from what my body is doing. The bodily sensations I experience I call feeling scared or feeling mad.

Admittedly, my brain probably orchestrated this set of sensations I call fear, so that my brain organizes what my body does. Long ago William James suggested that we do not cry because we feel sorry but that we feel sorry because we cry. In the same way there is truth in the suggestion that my heart does not beat because I am afraid but that my fear consists of a beating heart and trembling fingers.

So I insist that mind cannot be compared easily with body unless we recognize that it belongs to a different order of reality. Mind is not a thing so much as an "ing"—a feel*ing*, a remember*ing*, a know*ing*, a think*ing*, a decid*ing* and so on. Mind is what body does, in fact it is what body goes on doing all my life, even when I am asleep.

So to ask, "Where is mind?" is rather like asking where the concerto is when the orchestra has stopped playing. Mind, in one sense, isn't anywhere. Like an idea, it is not limited to a particular time or place.

Two further questions arise. Am I saying mind is not a real thing? Of course not. Function is real. But let us dig deeper. What happens to the mind when the body dies? If the body ceases to function at death, then logically mind must cease. Materialists nod eagerly. As Christians we do not agree. We may be baffled by what souls beneath the altar may experience (Rev 6:9-11), as baffled as we are about the relation between our experience of time and the experience of eternity. But two things are certain. We shall survive, even when stripped of our bodies. More importantly, our permanent state will remain a bodily one. We are to be raised from the dead bodily. Any bodyless state will be but temporary. The explanation of how this is so eludes us not because we are illogical but because we are incapable at this point of experiencing eternity.

A second question. A sentence or two back I talked about being stripped of my body. In so speaking I imply that I am more than my body. What am "I"? Am I my mind? Or to put it another way, Is my mind the real me?

I am not sure whether I know the answer to the question. Some thinkers have suggested that I am not my mind because "I" can observe what is going on in my mind. My mind is merely a part of me that I am observing. But to think in such terms is to reintroduce the dichotomy we are trying to avoid. What some people call the observing ego is surely a part of the mind, and therefore a part of the bodily function. Second, like my mind, I too am something my body does or produces. I "arise from" my body, so to speak. And just as music is more than the orchestra that plays it, so "I" am more than my body. "I" am the whole which is more than the sum of my parts. By the same token I am not intended to have any permanent existence apart from a body, albeit a resurrection body. Just as the concerto needs the orchestra to play it into being, so I shall need, if I am to sing God's praises for eternity, a resurrection body as the basis of my being.

Alexander and Selesnick in their *History of Psychiatry* make the comment, "Three basic trends in psychiatric thought can be traced back to earliest times: (1) the attempt to explain diseases of the mind in physical terms, that is, the organic approach: (2) the attempt to find a psychological explanation for mental disturbances: and (3) the attempts to deal with inexplicable events by magic."[4] If Alexander and Selesnick are referring to demonic exorcism when they use the phrase *by magic,* we are still where we were in the earliest times. We still try to explain troubled behavior on a physical basis, on a psychological basis or on a demonic basis.

Now if mind is a function of body it will seem clear that malfunctions of my body can lead to malfunctions of my mind. Therefore "mental" conditions may perhaps have a physical explanation. Or can they? The question is not so simple. In saying that mind is a function of body we are using an analogy. The analogy is helpful. But it will have limitations. Clearly it is our daily experience that mind affects body just as much as body affects mind. If I have a toothache and have not slept for three nights, my bodily state will induce a mood of gloom that cripples my patience and my concentration alike. Bodily ills do in fact lead to mental distress.

Alternatively, if by use of my mind I discover that I am facing trouble (like losing my job for instance), I might suffer physically. I might lose my appetite or develop a peptic ulcer. It would seem that the mind-function model may oversimplify matters. At any rate it must be clear to us that it is just as true to say that matter influences function as to say that function influences matter, or, in simple terms, body affects mind just as mind affects body.

It is interesting to read the works of systems theorists and to discover that the same holds true for many complex systems. Take a telephone system for instance. I am assured by people who know much more about the matter than I do that when a telephone system—a mere conglomeration of wires, radio transmitters and devices I hold to my ear—reaches a certain size and degree of complexity, it begins to assume properties and characteristics that no one had anticipated. It takes on itself, as it were, a character of its own. To the dismay of its designers and operators and the fury of its users, it may even by its contrary whimsicality impair the physical components that make it up. It should not therefore surprise us that mind can indeed take priority at times over matter.

For *function* is a very poor word to describe that marvelous thing called mind.

Let us then be clear that there is a two-way street between mind and body. Each affects the other. Body affects mind, and mind affects body. Some would argue that mind affects body more than body affects mind. Among them are Christian Scientists, some psychoanalysts and a lot of fuddle-headed idealists. As human beings we prefer to think this way. Somehow it makes us feel more noble, more in control. But a simple blow on the head can obliterate the function of mind for days on end. A better case can be made, in my view, for the greater influence of body over mind. Certainly I long for a resurrection body. I know it will do far more for my mind than this one does.

Quietists and Activists

There is one more question to be addressed before we look at the nature of depression. If the Fall has made us vulnerable to sin, suffering and sickness, yet if at the same time we are redeemed servants of Christ, what should our stance be when trouble comes tumbling down over us? What attitude in particular should we adopt to our depressions and to the depressions of others?

Two extreme views have been taught through the ages. One is that we submit to all suffering, sickness, pain—whether mental or physical—as from God. We accept them as reality and take no action against them. Because they come to us from the hand of God we must yield without resistance, trusting the goodness of God who sends them, praising him for doing so, indeed "kissing the hand that wounds us." Since the evil is planned for our perfection, we must lie still in the Potter's hand.

Such views in their most extreme form were exemplified by Quietism, a mystical movement within Catholicism in seventeenth-century France and Italy, arising from the writings of Miguel de Molinos. It is known best to English readers by translations of the works of Fénelon and of Madame Guyon. Eventually, it was condemned as heresy by the Roman Catholic Church. The influence upon evangelicals has been profound and elements of Quietism are found in German Pietism, Quakerism and the Keswick movement.

Guyon's poems have been translated into English, some in the form of hymns.

> Long plunged in sorrow, I resign
> My soul to that dear hand of thine,
> *Without reserve or fear* [her italics]:
> That hand shall wipe my streaming eyes:
>   Or into smiles of glad surprise
>   Transform the falling tear.

> My rapid hours pursue the course
> Prescribed them by Love's sweetest force.
>   And by thy sovereign will
> Without a wish to escape my doom
> Though still a sufferer from the womb,
>   And doom'd to suffer still.[5]

The ultimate object of such passive yielding is the death of the natural man, a fifth stage in a progression of six degrees of holiness described in one of Fénelon's letters. The Christian's passive acceptance in faith of every suffering finally achieves this death, and death in turn is followed by life in union with God. Fénelon supposes that Paul was writing of such an exalted state when he wrote, "It is no longer I who live, but Christ who lives in me" (Gal 2:20).

The appeal of Quietism springs from its offer of release from tension and its offer of perfection through continuous bowing in faith and love to the will of God. The soul must take no action internally or externally but submit passively to the will of God. The danger of the doctrine lies in the idea that evil comes directly from God and that perfection comes via passive faith, and in the doctrine's inadequate grasp of justification.

At the other extreme from Quietism is a view espoused by those I call Activists. They believe that through the exercise of faith and by the power of Jesus' name we can banish every sickness, every difficulty. Sickness, tragedy, pain must be resisted, for all come from Satan. Indeed the "reality" of every evil, every problem must be rejected. Christians need not and must not ever be downcast. Unhappiness is a sign of defeat and unbelief. Any resort to the help of ungodly physicians (and more particularly psychologists and psychiatrists) is a tacit admission that the resources in Christ and in Scripture are inadequate.

I referred to the views as opposites. They differ in their understanding of the source of pain, so that one calls for a militant faith that dismisses pain and gloom whereas the other recommends passive acceptance of them. But both views also have much in common. Both are simplistic about the problem of pain. Both represent a mixture of truth and error. Both appeal to faith, seek to exalt God and call for obedience to his commands. Both call for an attitude of praise in the face of difficulties—the one that the glory of Christ will frustrate our deadly foe, the other that the Divine Surgeon's knife might cut away rotting carnality to the point of killing forever the natural man. Both call for faith rather than for thinking through "natural" solutions and taking steps to overcome pain. There is truth, important truth, in both.

Yet there is error in both as well. The error of the Quietists lies in the view that all suffering originates in God and that therefore no active steps should be taken against it. To do so would be to deny God his working. But the suffering that God permits is not necessarily meant to be welcomed with open arms. Nor is the road to holiness *primarily* one of personal suffering. The error of the Activists is their belief that faith in God will force God's hand. It will not.

How then should Christians respond to pain? There is a sense in which all pain comes to us from God. "Does evil befall a city, unless the LORD has done it?" Amos asks (3:6). By *evil* Amos means disaster (but disaster at the hands of evil men). Though God is not the author of evil, he so controls the sinful actions of his foes that evil is used to work justice, judgment, discipline and chastisement, most especially for those he loves. "Surely the wrath of men shall praise thee; the residue of wrath thou wilt gird upon thee," sang Asaph, the musician and poet (Ps 76:10). God would not be God if he were not in control of the spread of evil, and if he were not able to use it to defeat and destroy itself. Are the Quietists right then? Perhaps we should not resist evil. In Hebrews 12 we are exhorted in fact to regard it as chastening from God which we must endure (vv. 5-11). Everything depends, of course, on what we mean by *resistance*.

I am knocked down by a hit-and-run driver and sustain multiple fractures. An injury to my spine paralyzes me from the waist down. I am told by the surgeons that all may not be lost and that surgical intervention may restore my useless limbs. Some extreme Quietists would urge me to let God work his perfect will in my life through tragedy. The extreme activist would urge me to trust God, and not the surgeon, for healing.

The biblical position (or so it seems to me) lies somewhere between the two. I must certainly believe that somewhere in this terrible tragedy God has a purpose for me. He knew before the world began that it would happen. It happened with his express consent. But since he is not a cruel God, but a tender Father, he cannot have permitted so cruel a blow without some greater good in mind.

But through surgeons, be they godly or ungodly, he offers me hope that the trial may be short-lived. If God (who controls the actions of surgeons just as much as those of hit-and-run drivers) places help in my way, I must take the help offered as coming from his hand.

The real difficulty arises when we are not dealing with surgeons and hit-and-run drivers but with our moods, our emotions, our internal struggles. Indeed these are the sufferings which preoccupy the Quietists most of all. I must not resist the turmoil in my soul but recognize that God will in his own time remove it. Any endeavors on my part will interfere with what God is doing.

A further difficulty arises when there is nothing I can do about the tragedy that befalls me. The surgeons who examine me following my accident may offer me no hope. They may tell me that my spinal cord has been severed and can never be repaired. At this point I may be in greater danger from the Activists than from the Quietists. If there is nothing that doctors can do, I face one of two choices. Either I may accept my fate, shaken badly, but still counting on the goodness of God who must have some larger purpose in mind, or else I may regard my tragedy as a blow from the Enemy, claim victory in the name of Christ, and trust God for supernatural healing.

God still heals miraculously. But not always. Nor is it necessarily our faith that decides the issue, but his own larger purposes. When tragedy strikes, our first response should be to ask God what he requires of us. Faith for a miracle or trust in the face of tragedy?

Once when I was a medical student I was told by our family physician that my mother had a serious heart problem, and there was every possibility that she would soon die. There was nothing more he could do. As I prayed about the matter I had the impression—purely a subjective one—that I was to trust God to heal her. For the next two weeks I refused every fantasy that had to do with funerals and bereavement, adopting a rigorous posture of expectancy. Yet my mother's life continued to ebb away. One night it seemed that she must be dying. With labored breathing she could only gasp and whisper, "If only I could rest." I found somewhere to be alone and simply said, "If you intend to do it, Lord, it's got to be now!" In less than five minutes I returned to my mother's side. She was no longer distressed. In a clear, firm voice she asked, "You've been praying, haven't you?" Within a week she was well.

I do not explain such facts, I only record them. I have personally known miraculous intervention on other occasions, as though I were caught up in divine activity which was larger than myself. But it has been the exception, not the rule. Usually I have had no such prompting. Sometimes, in spite of not experiencing such a prompting, I have prayed "in faith" over the sick person. But in such cases nothing has happened. The critical question would seem to be one of being in step with the purposes of God. And so far as pain, suffering and sickness are concerned, his specific purposes for specific people are just that—*specific*.

The alternatives presented by Quietism and Activism have the virtue of being absolute. There is no room for ifs and buts, only for a rule. Suffering must always be accepted by faith or else always be overcome by faith. But in simplifying matters they can lead us into unreality, into creating a God who is consistent with our particular theology. And God will be what he will be. (Aslan is not a tame lion, as C. S. Lewis wrote.) It is better for us to be bewildered and uncomprehending, to confess that his ways confound us, than to hang so obstinately to our theories that we begin idolatrous worship of a God of our own creating.

Now it seems that in what might be called our interior life (in our feelings, our moods, our inner suffering), we can do something about pain. We are not usually helpless victims of the hot winds that blow across our souls nor of icy winds that freeze them. It also seems that the better our grasp of

Scripture and of the gospel of God's grace, the greater will be our capacity to deal with inner pain. (Two books of particular help in this regard are thirteen sermons of William Bridge, preached in London in 1648, now published by The Banner of Truth under the title *A Lifting Up for the Downcast*, and Martyn Lloyd-Jones's *Spiritual Depression*.)

Yet both Scripture and two thousand years of Christian experience warn us that the usual is not the invariable, that thick curtains of darkness may descend over our minds when nothing we can do will bring a ray of light. They may do so with or without any obvious cause. Job, David, Jeremiah, Martin Luther, John Bunyan, William Cowper and Charles Haddon Spurgeon are a few of the more illustrious names among thousands upon thousands of God's people who have suffered such darkness. So thick may be the darkness that prayer dies on our lips. The heavens are sealed. Truth becomes the mockery of meaningless words.

Amid this agony, it is time for me to take up the central question of this book: Can depression be a physical illness? Is it a disease of the mind or of the body?

I may be asking the wrong questions. If impaired matter functions badly and if an impaired function may boomerang to impair the matter it arises from, if bodily ills affect mental distress and mental distress affects the body, ought not our question to be more practical? How best can we help the depressed person? Psychologically? Spiritually? Physically?

It is here we need the utmost caution and humility. For as we saw at the beginning of the book, depression is not one thing but many, and the way we alleviate it will demand that we develop a profound insight not only into its nature but into the heart of the depressed person. No surgery is so delicate as that of mind. Unfortunately we too often move into it with clumsy clichés, with subtly damning exhortations, breezy banalities, and the latest idiocy in pop psychology. Or else with unnecessary pills.

Part II
Science
& the Masks

4
Saints, Science & Psychology

They apply pigeons, to draw the vapors
from the head. John Donne,
Devotions

There is a love-hate relationship between Christians and science. We fear science yet we worship it. If science "discovers" something that threatens Scripture or, which is much more likely, that threatens our favorite interpretation of Scripture, then science becomes the Enemy. Parents protest against the way it is taught in schools. We busily create Christian schools and Christian universities for which, embarrassingly, we need to import Christian professors trained in godless universities. On the other hand, if science discovers something that supports our favorite interpretations of Scripture, we discard our hostility and hail science as the latest and most reliable champion of the faith. After all, if science proves the Bible, the Bible must be true.

Most of us understand little about science, have too great a respect for it and overestimate its power both to undermine and to build up our faith. Science has little power to do either. It is true that some teachers of science use "scientific" arguments against faith, just as some Christians use "scientific" arguments to "prove" faith. But teachers of science and Christian apologists are human beings, and it is their human insecurity which sometimes is at work, not their scientific aptitudes.

Science is simply a useful way of looking at certain problems. It is limited in scope. It cannot bring about world peace, remove death or "discover" God. And while its application may add to the available supply of goods and services, it can do little to see that they are equitably distributed.

Of Fear and Faith

The love-hate relation between science and saints is especially noticeable in the human sciences. As a first-year psychiatric resident sitting in an adult Bible class in a church in Winnipeg, I squirmed under a long tirade by a visiting Bible expositor (did he really not know I was there?) about the evils of psychiatry. Rather pompously he told us that one could be a Christian. One could be a psychiatrist. But one could not be both a Christian and a psychiatrist at the same time. Not ever. Occasionally, I still hear such remarks, but they are growing fewer.

For now the psychologies fascinate us. Counseling is in. Young men and women preparing for the Christian ministry will do well to study psychology. They are likely to get better paying jobs with superior kinds of churches and have better prospects for an ecclesiastical career. I do not say that such should be their motive for studying psychology. I am simply pointing out the way things are. Pastors are frustrated by the perplexing family problems their church members bring them. It is a relief to be able to turn to an expert, and it is only natural to feel that what the church needs is more psychology.

But once again we fear psychology too much, and we expect

too much of it. And we do so in part because we have lost confidence in the Christian gospel, however much we profess to believe it. Consequently, we are too prone to pass on difficult cases to obliging counselors, social workers and psychologists without carefully considering whether we are doing so merely to get rid of a problem we ought to have been able to solve. There are times when pastors and elders should refer members of their flock to mental health professionals, but I have a growing fear of the role of psychology in the church and of its tendency to infringe on godly counsel.

The human sciences are still cutting their teeth. They are crowded with unproved (and sometimes unprovable) hypotheses and conflicting theories. Professional counselors, psychologists, psychiatrists and social workers can bring to their work a zeal for their particular beliefs which is more religious in character than scientific.

They are only human. Give a human being a little knowledge, especially if the knowledge enables him or her to belong to a prestigious group, and whether the knowledge is true or false, you get converts full of zeal for the "truth" you have imparted. Pour gentle contempt on other schools of thought and their teachings, and you will have them laughing with you.

But I would be doing the human sciences an injustice if I only painted one side of the picture. At the core of the movements, dedicated investigators carry out painstaking studies. During the last fifteen or twenty years psychologists, sociologists and psychiatrists of various schools have been humbly learning one another's languages and paying careful heed to one another's results. Not all science is "science falsely so called."

Scientific truth, like any other truth, can be frightening. You have to follow facts wherever they lead you, and at times they may seem to lead you down dangerous byways. Christians and non-Christians alike find the process difficult, for though investigation will threaten all of us at different points, it will threaten all of us equally.

Christians need have no fear of science provided we remember three things. First, scientists are merely investigating the laws of our Creator. They sometimes make serious mistakes in their investigations and arrive at wrong conclusions. But if they pursue matters far enough, they can only find truth, for truth is all there is to find. But because scientists make mistakes, all scientific conclusions must be tentative. Sooner or later the most unshakable and the most firmly founded ideas crumble and fall.

Consequently, it matters little whether science supports Scripture or not. If today's science opposes, we need not fear for today's theory will be replaced by another tomorrow. By the same token it is unwise to rejoice in science's support of Scripture. Who are scientists that they presume to "confirm" the Word of the living God?

Finally, science is only one of many ways of discovering truth and has serious limitations. It becomes dangerous only when we worship it, that is, when we assume it is the high road to all understanding. It can offer us no help with life's deepest questions. (Why do I exist? Why is there a universe? Does life have any meaning? How can we determine what is important in life?)

The Tower of Babel

One of my psychiatric colleagues in Winnipeg, Dr. John Adamson, once wrote, "Psychiatry is an orderly body of ignorance." His view is a little extreme. I would prefer to say that psychiatry, like other human sciences, is a disorderly mass of truths, half-truths and wild ideas.

I am reminded of the Indian parable about the three blind men who discussed what an elephant was like. The one who grasped a leg decided the elephant was like a tree trunk while the one who seized the trunk was sure the elephant was like a snake and the one who felt its side said it was like a wall. Those of us (psychologists, social workers, psychiatrists, counselors of different kinds) who treat and counsel probably disagree with one another's views about depression for similar reasons. We are blind men grasping different parts of an elephant. Indeed we may be in a more confusing situation yet, for I suspect that a leopard and a bear have also been thrown into the arena to be pawed over and studied by us in our blindness. And all of us have become experts.

The problem with us experts is that we invent new technical words. Not only do we differ in our opinions, but we also speak to one another in different languages. Indignation is compounded by semantic confusion. We in the human sciences have built our own Tower of Babel. Mercifully, God is not interested in scattering us but in securing our harmonious collaboration. If this were not so, our task would be hopeless. Moreover there are signs in good universities that godly and ungodly researchers alike are beginning to perceive that other theories as well as their own may have a contribution to make. The elephant after all may be something more than a mere tree, and certainly much larger than a snake.

Our problem arises, as I tried to indicate in chapter one, because we use the term *depression* to mean different things. Some people think of grief following bereavement as depression. Freud's paper "Mourning and Melancholia" was an attempt to distinguish normal from abnormal grieving. Others may refer to the humiliation following failure and defeat, or to the petulant response of one whose expectations of others are never met. In some "depressions" the depressed persons may feel angry with themselves because it is sometimes easier to get mad at oneself than to alienate someone whose approval is important to us. "Depression" to other people may represent unresolved emotional problems.

I am concerned more with depression (whatever its type or origin) which has assumed graver and perhaps life-threatening proportions. The distinction between the "depressions" above and what I would like to call depressive illness is not always clear, but slowly patterns are beginning to emerge and to make more sense.

In general the more serious forms of depression (depressive illness) are treated by psychiatrists and clinical psychologists while the less malignant varieties are helped by counselors of many kinds. Some depressions probably receive medical treatment when they really need psychological or spiritual counseling while others who need medical treatment are treated by counselors. Some of the latter believe that depression should never be regarded as a medical or psychiatric illness, but their numbers are finally decreasing. Meanwhile, in good universities, human behavior departments, and brain research centers people are seeking to collaborate throughout the Western world with the World Health Organization in adopting a common language and more rigorous definitions of terms.

One of the most rigorous searches for clear definitions is a recent effort on the part of the American Psychiatric Association who have put out a manual known as *Diagnostic and Statistical Manual III* (DSM III). While it has ardent advocates and indignant opponents, it seems clearly the most comprehensive attempt yet to standardize the terminology used in all forms of mental illness, personality and behavior problems and to delineate with extreme care the precise boundaries separating different conditions. I have no doubt that the boundaries are going to get pushed around. But at least the Americans have made a valiant attempt to cope with the Tower of Babel confusion. Two research teams on opposite sides of the world can be reasonably sure that they understand what each other is saying if both use standard terms, such as those DSM III proposes.

My own contribution will be to share a simplified version of some recent classifications of depressive illnesses. Depressive (or affective) illnesses are currently divided into the basic categories shown in Figure 1.

Figure 1
Categories of Depressive Illness

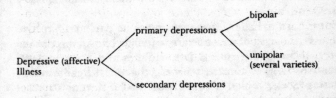

Primary depressions are mood disorders which are *not* associated with any other form of mental or physical illness, nor with conditions like alcoholism, homosexuality or the like. The distinction is made because we do not know the effect of physical illness on depression. It is best to be clear whether or not we are dealing with primary depressions (depression in "pure culture," so to speak).

Secondary depressions, on the other hand, are those which arise in the course of the illnesses or conditions mentioned.

Bipolar depressions are primary depressions which are characterized not only by plunges into despair but also by ascents into euphoria and even manic excitement. It is the illness that once was called manic-depressive psychosis.

Unipolar depressions (it is suspected that there are several varieties of these) do not combine highs as well as lows, but, as their name suggests, are plunges into darkness relieved only by elevation into normal moods.

To merit the description of depressive illness all of these conditions must last at least a month, and usually last much longer. All have a tendency toward spontaneous remission without any treatment after a period of time varying from several months even to a number of years. Occasionally a unipolar depression may be lifelong, or else there may be spontaneous remission only for a month or two each year, usually in the summer. Severe forms of bipolar illness are those in which the fluctuations from mania to melancholy are continuous.

It is hard to believe that stress plays no part in depressive illness since most of us are aware of feeling blue in response to overwhelming difficulties. Drs. Holmes and Rahe in 1967 went so far as to construct a scale, the Social Readjustment Rating Scale[1] which allotted scores to different stressful events. If you had undergone the stress of bereavement or been abandoned by your spouse or even if you had been buying a new home, you would have high stress scores. And if you were unfortunate enough to acquire more than 300 points on the Holmes-Rahe Scale in a twelve-month period, you would be a risk for depression or another breakdown.

Most of the evidence currently seems to go against Holmes and Rahe.[2] Life events may make us unhappy and put us under a sense of strain, but in and of themselves would not seem to produce depressive illness.

I indicated earlier that the boundaries separating depressed feelings caused by external circumstances from depressive illness with physical causes are far from clear. Later I hope to give full descriptions of the illnesses, but the question arises as to whether there are tests of any kind by which the illnesses may be measured or classified. Is there any scientific approach to them? Can we qualify them and attach numbers to them? Are there biochemical tests or blood tests to distinguish one kind from another? Are there psychological tests to help us assess them?

The answer to all the questions is yes. Some tests, whether biochemical or psychological, are simple and easily administered. Others are complex, time-consuming and expensive.

Some are available only as research tools at present. The big question is, How trustworthy are they? Do they measure what they are supposed to measure? How useful are they?

Measurement and Numbers

Lord Kelvin once said, "When you can measure what you are speaking about, and express it in numbers you know something about it, but when you cannot express it in numbers, your knowledge is of a meagre and unsatisfactory kind: it may be knowledge but you have scarcely, in your thoughts, advanced to the stage of science, whatever the matter may be."[3]

Not everyone would agree with Lord Kelvin. Some kinds of knowledge do not lend themselves to measurement. Certainly it is more difficult to measure human psychological attributes than it is to measure things in physics or chemistry or astronomy.

Some people would say that the science model used by physicists and chemists is unsuitable for the human sciences, and they may be right. Yet for better or worse we are stuck for want of a better model with the one that has served physics and chemistry, a model which depends on numbers, tables, graphs and mathematics.

Perhaps it is better than nothing. But we must be cautious. Both numbers and names can create the illusion that we know something. The name *black hole* in astronomy gives us a sense of knowing what black holes are, yet we can only make conjectures about what goes on inside a black hole. Numbers, like names, can lend a false sense of precision to an argument. When we talk of measuring, most of us have rulers or tape measures in the back of our minds. Rulers are made to conform to certain standards (originally set in stone and kept in scientific institutes at controlled temperatures), and people who use rulers a great deal get to be fairly accurate in their measurements. In the human sciences, however, we have to measure things that by their very nature are elusive, such as personality traits, degrees of mental illness, the effectiveness of psychotherapy or of a given psychotherapist. An enormous amount of thought has been put into developing measuring instruments that can be used in a scientific approach to human problems. On the whole they have benefited us by forcing us to give up cherished fables, to be more disciplined in our observations and in our thinking, and by enabling one worker to compare his or her work with that of another worker.

We nevertheless must be cautious about taking measuring instruments too seriously. It is probably still true that the best measuring instrument is a human being—a well-trained, experienced person who can be both empathic and objective in assessing other human beings. I am deeply convinced that good novelists, for instance, are better judges of human nature than good psychologists, sociologists or psychiatrists.

The common objection to using ourselves as instruments is that in doing so we are relying upon our subjective feelings. Most of us have been brainwashed into believing that objective is superior to subjective—the former being accurate and dependable; the latter, imprecise and unreliable. What is true is that my subjective impressions will not always agree with yours. Therefore at least one set of subjective impressions is unreliable. Yet all of us would agree that some people exercise better (subjective) judgment than others. Our everyday lives are lived by trusting people whose judgment is better than our own.

The psychiatrists and psychologists who use themselves as instruments are not relying solely on their subjective impressions, but also on experience, both their accumulated store of experience, and experience garnered over many generations by their predecessors and passed down in the form of lectures, textbooks and other training devices.

Problems arise when one researcher carries out a study on depressed patients and another researcher wishes to repeat the study with another group of depressed patients. The results of the second study may differ from those of the first study. One reason for the difference may lie in the fact that in the first study the patients were more depressed than in the second. Both workers may have used similar terms *(severely depressed* or *psychotic depressions)* yet their criteria for using the terms may have differed.

At this point rating scales come to our rescue by supplementing our verbal description of our patients with numbers. If we can say that patients in a study scored an average of twenty points on Beck's Inventory then another group of investigators, checking on the results of our study, can also use the Beck Inventory to make their comparison meaningful.

Probably the five most frequently used scales for depression are Beck's Inventory for Measuring Depression, Zung's Self-Rating Depression Scale, The 'D' (Depression) Scale of the Minnesota Multiphasic Personality Inventory (MMPI) and the Hamilton Rating Scale for Depression. Each has advantages and disadvantages, strengths and weaknesses.

Beck's Inventory for Measuring Depression.[4] Aaron T. Beck constructed his inventory on attitudes and symptoms of depressed patients which he divided into twenty-one categories. (See Figure 2.) One category, for example, is weight loss. Four statements accompany each category. The statements for weight loss are:

0. I haven't lost much weight, if any, lately.
1. I have lost more than 5 pounds.
2. I have lost more than 10 pounds.
3. I have lost more than 15 pounds.

The severity of the depression is calculated by adding the numbers of the statements selected by the patient. Thus a patient who has lost more than 15 pounds would score 3

Figure 2
Beck's Inventory for Measuring Depression

A/0   I do not feel sad.
1   I feel sad.
2   I am sad all the time and I can't snap out of it.
3   I am so sad or unhappy that I can't stand it.

B/0   I am not particularly discouraged about the future.
1   I feel discouraged about the future.
2   I feel I have nothing to look forward to.
3   I feel that the future is hopeless and that things cannot improve.

C/0   I do not feel like a failure.
2   As I look back on my life, all I can see is a lot of failures.
1   I feel I have failed more than the average person.
3 ·   I feel I am a complete failure as a person.

D/0   I get as much satisfaction out of things as I used to.
1   I don't enjoy things the way I used to.
2   I don't get real satisfaction out of anything anymore.
3   I am dissatisfied or bored with everything.

E/0   I don't feel particularly guilty.
1   I feel guilty a good part of the time.
2   I feel quite guilty most of the time.
3   I feel guilty all of the time.

F/0   I don't feel I am being punished.
1   I feel I may be punished.
2   I expect to be punished.
3   I feel I am being punished.

G/0   I don't feel disappointed in myself.
1   I am disappointed in myself.
2   I am disgusted with myself.
3   I hate myself.

H/0   I don't feel I am any worse than anybody else.
1   I am critical of myself for my weaknesses or mistakes.
2   I blame myself all the time for my faults.
3   I blame myself for everything bad that happens.

I/0   I don't have any thoughts of killing myself.

1   I have thoughts of killing myself, but I would not carry them out.
2   I would like to kill myself.
3   I would kill myself if I had the chance.

J/0   I don't cry any more than usual.
1   I cry more now than I used to.
2   I cry all the time now.
3   I used to be able to cry, but now I can't cry even though I want to.

K/0   I am no more irritated now than I ever am.
1   I get annoyed or irritated more easily than I used to.
2   I feel irritated all the time now.
3   I don't get irritated at all by the things that used to irritate me.

L/0   I have not lost interest in other people.
1   I am less interested in other people than I used to be.
2   I have lost most of my interest in other people.
3   I have lost all of my interest in other people.

M/0   I make decisions about as well as I ever could.
1   I put off making decisions more than I used to.
2   I have greater difficulty in making decisions than before.
3   I can't make decisions at all any more.

N/0   I don't feel I look any worse than I used to.
1   I am worried that I am looking old or unattractive.
2   I feel that there are permanent changes in my appearance that make me look unattractive.
3   I believe that I look ugly.

O/0   I can work about as well as before.
1   It takes an extra effort to get started at doing something.
2   I have to push myself very hard to do anything.
3   I can't do any work at all.

P/0   I can sleep as well as usual.
1   I don't sleep as well as I used to.
2   I wake up 1-2 hours earlier than usual

and find it hard to get back to sleep.

eating less. Yes _____ No _____

3 I wake up several hours earlier than I used to and cannot get back to sleep.

Q/0 I don't get more tired than usual.

1 I get tired more easily than I used to.

2 I get tired from doing almost anything.

3 I am too tired to do anything.

R/0 My appetite is no worse than usual.

1 My appetite is not as good as it used to be.

2 My appetite is much worse now.

3 I have no appetite at all any more.

S/0 I haven't lost much weight, if any, lately.

1 I have lost more than 5 pounds.

2 I have lost more than 10 pounds.

3 I have lost more than 15 pounds.
I am purposely trying to lose weight by

T/0 I am no more worried about my health than usual.

1 I am worried about physical problems such as aches and pains; or upset stomach; or constipation.

2 I am very worried about physical problems and it's hard to think of much else.

3 I am so worried about my physical problems that I cannot think about anything else.

U/0 I have not noticed any recent change in my interest in sex.

1 I am less interested in sex than I used to be.

2 I am much less interested in sex now.

3 I have lost interest in sex completely.

Reprinted by permission from the University of Pennsylvania Press. Copyright 1967.

---

points. The Inventory is presented in a standardized manner and the total score measures the severity of the depression.

Zung's Self-Rating Depression Scale,[5] as its name implies, can be filled out by patients themselves. (See Figure 3.) Based on factor analysis (clustering) of patients' symptoms, and finding the commonest expressions patients used to express the clusters turned up by factor analysis, the scale consists of twenty statements, ten worded positively and ten worded negatively. Beside the statements are four columns headed "A Little of the Time," "Some of the Time," "A Good Part of the Time" and "Most of the Time." On negative questions the scoring allots one point for "A Little of the Time" and an additional point for each succeeding column. Thus "A Good Part of the Time" would score 3 points. On positive questions the scoring is reversed. Thus a patient who felt "down-hearted and blue" most of the time, and whose mornings felt good only a little of the time would score 8 points on the first two questions.

The MMPI is a much more complex instrument designed to help in the diagnosis not only of depression but of other forms

Figure 3
Key for Scoring Zung's Self-Rating Depression Scale

	A Little of the Time	Some of the Time	A Good Part of the Time	Most of the Time
1. I feel down-hearted and blue	1	2	3	4
2. Morning is when I feel the best	4	3	2	1
3. I have crying spells or feel like it	1	2	3	4
4. I have trouble sleeping at night	1	2	3	4
5. I eat as much as I used to	4	3	2	1
6. I still enjoy sex	4	3	2	1
7. I notice that I am losing weight	1	2	3	4
8. I have trouble with constipation	1	2	3	4
9. My heart beats faster than usual	1	2	3	4
10. I get tired for no reason	1	2	3	4
11. My mind is as clear as it used to be	4	3	2	1
12. I find it easy to do the things I used to	4	3	2	1
13. I am restless and can't keep still	1	2	3	4
14. I feel hopeful about the future	4	3	2	1
15. I am more irritable than usual	1	2	3	4
16. I find it easy to make decisions	4	3	2	1
17. I feel that I am useful and needed	4	3	2	1
18. My life is pretty full	4	3	2	1
19. I feel that others would be better off if I were dead	1	2	3	4
20. I still enjoy the things I used to	4	3	2	1

of emotional illness and personality disorders. It is filled out by the patient and has a built-in lie scale to detect any tendency to give untrue answers.

The Hamilton Rating Scale for Depression[6] demands skilled administration and two experienced raters, who rate it independently. Unlike Zung, Hamilton mistrusts the patient's own judgment and feels that an experienced expert is better. Like Zung, he constructs his scale by using factor analysis to group patients' symptoms into a twenty-one-item scale. (See Figure 4.)

How reliable are the scales? Do they accurately reflect the seriousness of someone's depression? If all are equally reliable, obviously it would be better to choose the Zung scale, which is carried out by the patient, is simple and takes no professional time. Failing that, one could use Beck's Inventory, which does call for administration by someone who is experienced, though it is short and easily interpreted.

A recent study tried to compare all the scales I have mentioned.[7] The scales were used on 155 patients (97 women and 58 men), successive admissions to the Hotel Dieu in Kingston, Ontario. The study confirmed what many workers feel (even those inventing scales), that "clinical examination and rating scales are best viewed, and used, as complementary to one another." The Hamilton Scale, though time-consuming and therefore expensive, clearly justified itself in being more sensitive to degrees of depression and clearly able to distinguish different diagnostic categories.

The Beck and Zung scales were unable to distinguish between transient situational reactions (temporary emotional upsets arising out of circumstances) and serious depression. In fact both scales gave slightly higher scores to people with transient situational reactions. Again, on the Zung scale people with character disorders scored higher (more depressed) than those judged by experienced psychiatrists to be profoundly depressed. Age and sex also affected both the

Figure 4
Hamilton Rating Scale for Depression

1. **Depressed Mood** (*Sad, hopeless, helpless, worthless*)
   - ☐ 0 = Absent
   - ☐ 1 = These feeling states indicated only on questioning
   - ☐ 2 = These feeling states spontaneously reported verbally
   - ☐ 3 = Communicates feeling states non-verbally—i.e., through facial expression, posture, voice, and tendency to weep
   - ☐ 4 = Patient reports VIRTUALLY ONLY these feeling states in his spontaneous verbal and non-verbal communication

2. **Feelings of Guilt**
   - ☐ 0 = Absent
   - ☐ 1 = Self-reproach, feels he has let people down
   - ☐ 2 = Ideas of guilt or rumination over past errors or sinful deeds
   - ☐ 3 = Present illness is a punishment. Delusions of guilt
   - ☐ 4 = Hears accusatory or denunciatory voices and/or experiences threatening visual hallucinations

3. **Suicide**
   - ☐ 0 = Absent
   - ☐ 1 = Feels life is not worth living
   - ☐ 2 = Wishes he were dead or any thoughts of possible death to self
   - ☐ 3 = Suicide ideas or gesture
   - ☐ 4 = Attempts at suicide (*any serious attempt rates 4*)

4. **Insomnia Early**
   - ☐ 0 = No difficulty falling asleep
   - ☐ 1 = Complains of occasional difficulty falling asleep—i.e., more than ½ hour
   - ☐ 2 = Complains of nightly difficulty falling asleep

5. **Insomnia Middle**
   - ☐ 0 = No difficulty
   - ☐ 1 = Patient complains of being restless and disturbed during the night
   - ☐ 2 = Waking during the night—any getting out of bed rates 2 (*except for purposes of voiding*)

6. **Insomnia Late**
   - ☐ 0 = No difficulty
   - ☐ 1 = waking in early hours of the morning but goes back to sleep
   - ☐ 2 = Unable to fall asleep again if he gets out of bed

7. **Work and Activities**
   - ☐ 0 = No difficulty
   - ☐ 1 = Thoughts and feelings of incapacity, fatigue or weakness related to activities: work or hobbies
   - ☐ 2 = Loss of interest in activity: hobbies or work—either directly reported by patient, or indirect in listlessness, indecision and vacillation (*feels he has to push self to work or activities*)
   - ☐ 3 = Decrease in actual time spent in activities or decrease in productivity. In hospital, rate 3 if patient does not spend at least three hours a day in activities (*hospital job or hobbies*) exclusive of ward chores
   - ☐ 4 = Stopped working because of present illness. In hospital, rate 4 if patient engages in no activities except ward chores, or if patient fails to perform ward chores unassisted

8. **Retardation** (*Slowness of thought and speech; impaired ability to concentrate; decreased motor activity*)
   - ☐ 0 = Normal speech and thought
   - ☐ 1 = Slight retardation at interview
   - ☐ 2 = Obvious retardation at interview
   - ☐ 3 = Interview difficult
   - ☐ 4 = Complete stupor

9. **Agitation**
   - ☐ 0 = None
   - ☐ 1 = Fidgetiness
   - ☐ 2 = Playing with hands, hair, etc.
   - ☐ 3 = Moving about, can't sit still
   - ☐ 4 = Hand ringing, nail biting, hair-pulling, biting of lips

10. **Anxiety Psychic**
    - ☐ 0 = No difficulty
    - ☐ 1 = Subjective tension and irritability
    - ☐ 2 = Worrying about minor matters
    - ☐ 3 = Apprehensive attitude apparent in face or speech
    - ☐ 4 = Fears expressed without questioning

11. Anxiety Somatic
- □ 0 = Absent
- □ 1 = Mild
- □ 2 = Moderate
- □ 3 = Severe
- □ 4 = Incapacitating
  Physiological concomitants of anxiety, such as:
  Gastro-intestinal-*dry mouth, wind, indigestion, diarrhea, cramps, belching*
  Cardio-vascular-*palpitations, headaches*
  Respiratory-*hyperventilation, sighing*
  Urinary frequency
  Sweating

12. Somatic Symptoms Gastrointestinal
- □ 0 = None
- □ 1 = Loss of appetite but eating with staff encouragement. Heavy feelings in abdomen
- □ 2 = Difficulty eating without staff urging. Requests or requires laxatives or medication for bowels or medication for G.I. symptoms

13. Somatic Symptoms General
- □ 0 = None
- □ 1 = Heaviness in limbs, back or head. Backaches, headache, muscle aches. Loss of energy and fatigability
- □ 2 = Any clear-cut symptom rates 2

14. Genital Symptoms
- □ 1 = Absent
- □ 1 = Mild
- □ 2 = Severe
  Symptoms such as: Loss of libido
  Menstrual disturbances

15. Hypochondriasis
- □ 0 = Not present
- □ 1 = Self-absorption (bodily)
- □ 2 = Preoccupation with health
- □ 3 = Frequent complaints, requests for help, etc.
- □ 4 = Hypochondriacal delusions

16. Loss of Weight *Rate either A or B*
A. When Rating By History:
- □ 0 = No weight loss
- □ 1 = Probable weight loss associated with present illness
- □ 2 = Definite (according to patient) weight loss
- □ X = Not assessed

B. On Weekly Ratings By Ward Psychiatrist, when Actual Weight Changes Are Measured:
- □ 0 = Less than 1 lb. weight loss in week
- □ 1 = Greater than 1 lb. weight loss in week
- □ 2 = Greater than 2 lb. weight loss in week
- □ X = Not assessed

17. Insight
- □ 0 = Acknowledges being depressed and ill
- □ 1 = Acknowledges illness but attributes cause to bad food, climate, overwork, virus, need for rest, etc.
- □ 2 = Denies being ill at all

18. Diurnal Variation
A. Note whether symptoms are worse in morning or evening. If NO diurnal variation, mark none
- □ 0 = No variation
- □ 1 = Worse in A.M.
- □ 2 = Worse in P.M.

B. When present, mark the severity of the variation. Mark "None" if NO variation
- □ 0 = None
- □ 1 = Mild
- □ 2 = Severe

19. Depersonalization and Derealization
- □ 0 = Absent
- □ 1 = Mild
- □ 2 = Moderate
- □ 3 = Severe
- □ 4 = Incapacitating
  Such as: *Feelings of Unreality*
  Nihilistic ideas

20. Paranoid Symptoms
- □ 0 = None
- □ 1 = Suspicious
- □ 2 = Ideas of reference
- □ 3 = Delusions of reference and persecution

21. Obsessional and Compulsive Symptoms
- □ 0 = Absent
- □ 1 = Mild
- □ 2 = Severe

Beck and the Zung scales, younger patients scoring higher. Females scored higher on the MMPI and males higher on the Beck. All in all the Hamilton seemed to be the most valuable though costliest instrument. What is also clear is that scales cannot at this stage replace experienced professionals and that the numbers garnered from scales do not represent infallible guides.

When Experiments Disagree

Perhaps you are beginning to understand some of the difficulties entailed in a scientific approach to depression. It may not surprise you to know that different groups of researchers carrying out similar studies often produce contradictory results and arrive at opposing conclusions. This is not such a bad thing as it may seem. The deficiencies of the first two studies will probably be rectified in the next six. Progress is slow but we learn by our mistakes. Unhappily, spectacular results (which may prove quite erroneous) get into the press. The unspectacular corrections to those same results are less newsworthy so that the general public is frequently left with a sort of potpourri of the latest and most spectacular fads.

Yet science, within its rather severe limitations, is useful. It has proved of great benefit to depressed patients, particularly in the last fifteen years. Christians should be wary of attaching the same value to scientific findings as to revealed truth, and should be extremely cautious about newspaper reports of spectacular advances. At the same time we should not dismiss science out of hand. Indeed, as we look into the discoveries of science, we should be impressed by the amazing workings of the human body and be inspired with awe at the wisdom of our Creator.

5
The Masks of Melancholy

The signs of approaching melancholy are . . . anguish and distress, dejections, silence, animosity . . . sometimes a desire to live and at other times a longing for death, suspicion on the part of the patient that a plot is being hatched against him. . . .
Caelius Aurelianus, fifth century A.D.

I'll change my state with any wretch
Thou canst from good or dungeon fetch
My pain's past cure, another Hell,
I may not in this torment dwell,
Now desperate I hate my life,
Lend me a halter or a knife,
*   All my griefs to this are jolly*
Naught so damned as melancholy.
Robert Burton, 1621, The Anatomy of Melancholy

I have made it clear that modern research suggests there are several depressive illnesses, distinguishable not only by their outward appearances and severity but also by their physiology and the biochemistry of their course. But it is time we lumped the illnesses together and described people who suffer from them. Most of the illnesses are unipolar. The sufferers become depressed but never elated. Bipolar illness, as its name suggests, differs from the rest so that the sufferer alternates between elation and despair.

Let me then try to describe depression and mania, at least to describe their many forms. For melancholy wears many masks. One person's depression can appear to be quite different from someone else's. You get a hint of depressions' variability from Aurelianus's fifth-century description, " . . . sometimes a desire to live and at other times a longing for death, suspicion on the part of the patient that a plot is being hatched against him . . ."

Depressions differ, yet as we have already seen they eventually have a good deal in common, sharing what physicians call "a final common pathway" and responding to similar kinds of treatment. But initially they come in a variety of shapes and sizes.

Differences arise because people are different. A hysterical person will become more hysterical or even hostile, an obsessive person more obsessive, a self-pitying person still more self-pitying and a suspicious person distinctly paranoid as the illnesses progress. Indeed in mild depressions the "nondepressive" symptoms may so predominate that the underlying condition is missed. Perhaps then we should look first at the many symptoms thought to be typical of a variety of depressions. Later we will also look at some of the special forms it takes and then in detail at the mania of bipolar illness.

The Mood and the Affect

Affect is a technical term used to describe a sustained *mood*. *Mood* represents the emotional weather ("I'm in a bad mood today") whereas *affect* represents the climate ("I keep getting this way. It's been going on for weeks now").

Depression is the outstanding affect from which depressive illness gets its name. Not all sufferers use the word. They may say things like "I feel down—discouraged," "I feel like giving up," "I'm always defeated," "I don't seem to be able to pray anymore," "God isn't real," "My prayers bounce off the ceiling," "I feel like I've been a failure all my life."

All of us experience such feelings from time to time. The solutions are many—a brisk walk, counting our blessings, a good night's sleep, talking with friends, a few hymns of praise, a time with God. When, however, the feelings continue to haunt us while weeks become months, we should turn to someone for help. "The researcher's task is to find out why most individuals undergo transient and minor fluctuations in response to everyday stresses, while 5% of men and women make one or several descents into the abyss of despair."[1]

Unfortunately, Christians tend to see their depressions only in spiritual terms. They feel they have let God down. Religious Jews do the same, interpreting their experiences from within a religious framework. And spiritual counselors, caught up in the same thought frame, may rightly diagnose a spiritual problem in one client but miss a depressive illness in another so that faith is encouraged when faith is impossible, or praise encouraged from a heart as withered as a prune.

I remember a gifted musician being dragged daily to the piano to play and sing songs of praise. "At first it would work," she told me. "At least for the time being I'd feel better. But as the weeks wore on it got worse and worse. In the end I hated the piano. I hated the hymns. *I just could not make my fingers play.*" Her symptoms were being treated while her illness was allowed to progress. While doctors frequently refer depressed Christians to me, pastoral counselors rarely do so. Perhaps they are less alert to the possibility of depressive illness. Some patients who have been receiving counseling for years have been made well in a couple of months once the real problem has been sorted out.

Along with the depressed affect, religious patients are plagued with feelings of guilt. Their knowledge of God's grace and mercy seems powerless to help them. They condemn themselves as lazy, as bad parents, as ungrateful spouses, as poor providers, as bad witnesses, as self-pitying and the like. They may "understand" the nature of God's forgiveness but lack any sense of it. Told to trust facts and not feelings, they struggle to obey but sometimes their troubled minds embrace ideas they have long resisted. They decide that they never were Christians or that they have committed the unpardonable sin. "All my friends tell me I'm a Christian," said a bewildered little lady the other day, "and I used to think I was myself. But I know now that I'm not."

Such patients often know neither joy nor pleasure. In the earlier stages of the illness there were things that they could enjoy—sunshine, a bouquet of flowers, a visit from a friend, a favorite piece of music, a day in the woods. But as matters progress patients may reach a total incapacity to experience pleasure in anything or anyone. We refer to the inability as *anhedonia*, a well-known depressive symptom.

Some may weep in solitude. One of my patients wakes at 3:00 A.M. daily and weeps until around 7:00 A.M. Others may wish to weep but find they are powerless to do so. To weep would be to experience relief. But their tear ducts have dried up. They can no longer cry.

"It Can't All Be in My Head!"

For many people *tiredness* rather than sadness is the principal symptom. Ever more weary with neither drive, energy, nor ambition they must force themselves to work. Many condemn themselves for their "laziness." People who watch them may notice a slowing of their movements. Their step has no alacrity, their speech no wit, their eyes no sparkle. They may consult a physician mentioning only their tiredness and be told after a careful physical examination and a series of tests (an examination that is essential before a diagnosis of depression can be entertained) that no physical basis can be found for their tiredness, no insidious infection, no anemia, no abnormality in thyroid function, nothing amiss with heart, lungs, bowel, no reason to suspect cancer. Unless both physicians and patients are alert to the weariness of depression, patients may leave the doctor's office convinced that something must be wrong, but what? And where can they go for help? To a psychologist or a psychiatrist? Not that! *"It can't be all in my head!"* they tell themselves.

With the tiredness there may also be a *sense of weakness*. "I feel weak. My arms are heavy. It can't be just my age!" some patients tell me.

Sometimes the physical slowing is so obvious that we speak of *psychomotor retardation*. A woman sits in my office, her face a picture of resignation. There is an unnatural stillness about her. I question her. There is a long pause. Then slowly, in a low tired voice she answers me with a word or two. She suffers from the psychomotor retardation of depression.

Curiously, the next depressed patient may show a very different picture. Instead of immobility he is painfully restless. His face is worried and he can scarcely stay in his chair. He repeats himself, fearful that I have not understood. Or else he sends me a barrage of questions. Will he get better? What am I going to do with him? How ever will he get out of the mess he is in? Am I going to lock him up? How long will it take him to get better? He wrings his hands. His anxious questions never cease and I can hardly get him out of my office for he clings to me, pulling me back to get more reassurance from me. He suffers from what we call an *agitated depression*. Agitation and psychomotor retardation are two sides of the coin of depression.

There may be *tension and anxiety*, anxiety about everything and about nothing at all, anxiety that was never there before. Or *fear*. Fear of death. Fear of tomorrow. Fear of people. Specific fears and vague ill-defined fears. Fears return to haunt them that once were easy to laugh away or to dismiss with robust faith.

"I *can't concentrate*," many patients tell me. "I read a page of a magazine and I've no idea what I've read. I haven't been able to enjoy reading for the last three months. I used to read all the time. And *my memory* seems to be failing. I just don't remember. . . ." Or else, "I *can't make decisions*. I can't make up my mind about anything—not even about the simplest things."

I marvel, in retrospect, at Dr. Emil Kraepelin's clinical acumen and the vivid descriptions he gives of the depressed patients he saw many years ago. The observations and opinions he recorded are being rediscovered after more than seventy years. It was Kraepelin who first observed the connection of mania and melancholia in the illness we now refer to as bipolar affective illness. No one has given so vivid and detailed descriptions either of mania or of melancholy.

> Thinking is difficult to the patient, a disorder which he describes in varied phrases. He cannot collect his thoughts or pull himself together; his thoughts are as if paralysed, they are immobile. His head feels heavy, quite stupid . . . He is no longer able to perceive, or to follow the train of thought of a book or a conversation, he feels weary, enervated, inattentive, inwardly empty; he has no memory; he has no command of knowledge formerly familiar to him, he must consider a long time about simple things. . . . He feels . . . "a creature disinherited of fate"; he is sceptical about God, and with a certain dull submission, which shuts out every comfort and every gleam of light, he drags himself with difficulty from one day to another.[2]

The descriptions continue for page after page and as I read his book I find myself populating it with patients I have known, patients who, were it not for the gap in time, he might well have been describing.

"I *can't face people,*" a young man told me today. When I travel I have to stay in people's homes. I didn't used to be like this, but now I hole up in my room all the time."

"I feel awkward in church," a depressed middle-aged woman complained. "I find I can't face people. I look for the quickest exit and pretend not to notice people coming toward me. I'm sort of ashamed—as though I know I'm going to make a fool of myself. And when someone does speak to me, I don't know what to say." Yet when she is well she delights in chatting with friends and strangers alike.

The symptoms that show the illness calls for medical measures are what are known as *hypothalamic symptoms,* symptoms related to the part of the brain, the hypothalamus, that regulates sleep, appetite, weight and sex. Again the patterns vary. In less serious depressions patients may either have difficulty getting to sleep (as all of us do at times) or else may sleep excessively. "I sleep to escape," some patients tell me. "I can shut everything out when I sleep." But in more serious depressions the pattern changes.

"How do you sleep?" I asked a middle-aged man.

"Oh, so-so."

"So-so?"

"Well, I get to sleep all right," he said warily, "but I waken around four in the morning. Generally I toss around for a while, but it's never any use. I get up—four-thirty, five maybe."

"And how d'you feel at that hour in the morning?"

He shook his head slowly. "Morning's the worst time."

"How long have you been waking that early?"

"Five months—perhaps six."

And there are sexual changes. A few men and women become obsessed with thoughts of sex, haunted by temptations that normally would be no problem. Some have affairs which bring no joy and only add to the weight of guilt they already feel. A recent issue of *Psychology Today* equated promiscuity in women with depression.[3] On the other hand, some men with happy marriages are suddenly overwhelmed with homosexual fantasies.

More commonly, sexual drive diminishes and sometimes disappears altogether. "Not interested." "Can't do it anymore. I wish I could for my wife's sake. I know she feels bad." "I hate it. Well, not actually *hate,* but I get nothing out of it." Whether with sleep or with sex, it is the change that is significant, the disruption of normal patterns and normal appetites.

There are also changes in appetite for food. As with sleep,

the less common pattern is to want more. The common pattern is to eat less.

"Do you enjoy your food?" I may ask.

"Well, no. Leastways not like I used to."

"How's your appetite then?"

"I don't seem to have any. I eat because I know I have to. And I'm constipated all the time."

"Lost any weight?"

It is then that I get answers that vary between five and fifty pounds of weight loss.

"Were you *trying* to lose weight—dieting?"

"No."

"How d'you know it's that much? Are you sure you're not mistaken?"

"My clothes are too big. My pants fall down. I've had to have them taken in."

Invariably I make sure a thorough physical examination is carried out. Again I must emphasize the importance of such an examination. Usually there is nothing to account for the weight loss but the depressive illness.

Some patients have another curious symptom that we call *diurnal mood variation*. Their mood gets a little better in the late afternoon or evening. Mornings may be intolerable. "It hits me as soon as my feet touch the floor and I say, 'Here it comes again.'" But as the day wears to a close, there is some relief. Things begin to look a little more hopeful (at least until dawn the next day). Curiously even the flow of the saliva in their mouths changes, switching to nighttime rates by day, and daytime rates by night. The brain's internal clocks no longer function properly.

At one time it was commonly taught in psychiatric textbooks that the onset both of unipolar and bipolar depression was in middle life. A first serious depression, for instance, was commonly believed to occur around the age of forty. But with more careful studies and better data collection increasing numbers of teen-agers are found to be depressed. Carlson and his colleagues note three different views common to psychiatrists regarding depression in adolescents:

1. that it is almost nonexistent;

2. that it exists, but in the form of "behavioral deviance" where aberrant behavior is called a "depressive equivalent"; and

3. that if investigated, all the adult characteristics of depression will be found (Carlson's own view).[4]

The author also found a family history of depression in many of the depressed adolescents.

Even children suffer depressive illness. Among my own patients I have noticed that depressed children's grades make a significant leap as their depression is healed.

Bipolar illness can also begin in or before adolescence. Of nine manic depressive patients who in retrospect were seen to have their first episode of mania before the age of sixteen, only one, Carlson noted, was correctly diagnosed at the time.

Camouflage Symptoms

Then there are the symptoms that mask the underlying depressive illness: *phobias, obsessions and compulsions*. I cannot recall reading about them in textbooks on depression or being taught about them in this context in my psychiatric training, but I began to stumble on them by accident.

Some years ago a thirty-three-year-old man came to see me about a problem which some psychiatrists would call a phobia, others an obsessive thought and others a compulsion. He was frightened that he was going to knock someone down with his car. Every day when he got home from work he had the feeling that he *might* have collided with a pedestrian. "It's usually when I turn a corner," he would tell me. "I can't be sure that I didn't see someone out of the corner of my eye. Or else I'll think I must have heard the car bang against someone —sort of sideswipe them."

"But you didn't actually hear the bump?"

"No, but, but *I couldn't be sure I didn't.* I know it's crazy—but I keep having to go back to make sure."

"You actually go back?"

"Pretty often. I get more and more worked up if I don't. Crazy, isn't it?"

He seemed tense, almost on the point of tears. He told me with shame that his sexual relations with his wife were not very good, that he "couldn't satisfy her" and that things were getting tense between them. Looking back I have no idea why it would have occurred to me to prescribe an antidepressant medication for him. But I did, and within five weeks he was well.

His wife was with him on that particular visit. Both wore smiles of grateful bewilderment. "It's gone—gone completely. I don't even think of it . . . well, it may just occur to me once in a while but I just brush it off," he told me. "And this thing between us," he glanced, half embarrassed, at his wife, "is O.K. now."

As we talked it became clear that he had been suffering from a moderately severe depressive illness masked by his obsession and his sexual difficulties. He continued for three months on the medication which was then withdrawn. When last I had contact with him he was still doing well. The point is not that medication cured him. The method of cure is relatively unimportant. What matters is that his obsessions were symptoms of depression.

I wish all obsessions were cured so easily. Not all are, and I have never taken the time to go through my records to analyze the number of phobic, obsessive or compulsive patients who have responded to antidepressant treatment. But the relation between these states and depressive illness is now receiving more general recognition.

In a recent study by David Sheehan and his colleagues[5] fifty-seven patients who had been severely disabled for an average period of thirteen years by agoraphobia, panic attacks, overwhelming fear and other phobias (conditions in which psychotherapy, behavior therapy and tranquilizing medication have all had at best only moderate success) were randomly assigned to three treatment groups. One group was treated by group psychotherapy, another by a monoamine oxidase inhibiting antidepressant (MAOI) and the third with tricyclic antidepressants (TCAs) (two different classes of antidepressant medication). Patients in the second and third groups showed very significant improvement over those in the first. Once again the point at issue is not the superiority of one treatment over another but that the crippling symptoms were presumably a reflection of an underlying depressive illness.

Another recent article explored the relation between depression and agoraphobia, a fear of public places which keeps people housebound.[6] I have seen a number of patients, with whom other methods of treatment have been only partially successful, set free from their housebound fears by antidepressant medication.

No obsessions can be more painful than persistent blasphemous and obscene thoughts and words that bombard the minds of some Christians. I recall a pastor who was tortured endlessly by his fear of blasphemy against the Holy Ghost. Calvinist by conviction, theologically sophisticated, his very sharp mind could see every side to every argument. He loved the Lord deeply. Yet his grip on reality became tenuous as sexual thoughts gripped his mind till he could not shut them out and blasphemous obscenities hemmed in his every effort to break free.

"How can I be a Christian when such thoughts control me?" He could anticipate each scriptural assurance I gave him and reinterpret it to his own damnation.

Satanic? Possibly, but if so, Satan was taking advantage of a sick body. After exploring the nature of and reasons for his condition and regulating his system by thorough antidepressant treatment, I helped control his problem. He could preach, enjoy his family and minister pastoral comfort to his flock. His obsessions were gone because the depression giving rise to them was effectively treated. While not all obsessions are related to depression, their presence should make the counselor alert to the possibility, for many of them are.

There is also the matter of hypochondriasis, excessive concern about one's health. Some patients are endlessly preoccupied with their bowels or their acne or their hearts. The concern is exaggerated when they become depressed. One old man I tried always (I am ashamed to say) to dodge as I passed through the ward. He would cling to me. What was I going to do with all the blood he was passing? (The nurses checked his specimens but couldn't find blood.) When was he going to see the ophthalmologist, the ENT specialist, the cardiologist, the gastroenterologist, the orthopedic surgeon and the neurologist? (He had seen them all more than once, and they too would dodge him when they saw him approach.) Didn't I know he had cancer of his kidneys, in his bowels and on his penis? What was I going to do to stop his going blind?

After vigorous antidepressant treatments he was calm, rational and told us that he felt great. His worries about his health had all disappeared. Again the method of treatment is not the issue, but the gross exaggeration of worry about his bodily health that arose from an underlying depression. Hypochondriasis had reached delusional proportions, which reminds me that depressed patients can indeed become psychotic. That is, they can lose touch with reality, become both delusional and subject to hallucinations.

Akiskal and Vahe[7] note that the kind of delusions from which depressed (or manic) patients suffer are usually understandable; that is, they are depressive or manic delusions. *Delusions of guilt* and sin and a sense of moral failure, or *imaginary poverty* and pessimism in men about their ability to provide for themselves and their families may accompany depression. There may also be *nihilistic delusions* such as ideas of one's bowels rotting away or that one is already dead. The paranoid delusions are essentially depressive in that the patient's imaginary persecutors are merely trying to inflict the punishment the sufferer believes he or she truly deserves.

I think of a fifty-six-year-old surgeon who was brought to the hospital from the countryside believing he had killed a patient on the operating table that afternoon. (The operation had been a difficult one, but the patient was recovering well.) The surgeon's wife told me that for weeks her husband had seemed extremely tired, had been uncommunicative and had discontinued his practice of assiduously reading professional journals.

He seemed profoundly depressed and fearful, shaking his head from time to time.

"You didn't kill your patient," I told him. "She's doing very well."

There was a long pause.

"How do you know?"

"I've talked with your partner."

"You're trying to cover up—you, my wife and my partner. I've made a mess of my life. I've sinned against God. I've ruined my family." No assurances of understanding that we could give him, no reminders about the mercy of God or of his family's well-being could reach him.

As days passed he became convinced that my sessions with him were covert interrogations designed to trap him into an admission of guilt. He was doomed. "You don't have to pretend," he told me. "I will gladly confess everything." His only fear was that his family would perish. (He still had teen-age children at home.) He was "bankrupt." He would never have the energy to earn his way out of debt because his strength was gone. His reputation was ruined and so on and so on.

My patient's delusions, like those mentioned previously, were what we call *mood congruent;* that is, they were the kind of delusions that go along with feelings of depression. The fact that they were mood congruent was one clue that his psychosis represented a serious form of depression and that they were not symptoms of an illness like schizophrenia. Once again, when we treated the depression, his delusions disappeared, his optimism returned and he is today enjoying a busy and successful practice.

Emil Kraepelin described this sort of depression: "The patient sees that he is surrounded by spies, is being followed by detectives, has fallen into the hands of a secret court of justice, of an avenging Nemesis, is going ... to prison ... to be slaughtered, executed, burned, nailed to the cross, all his teeth are being drawn out, his eyes dug out, he is innoculated with syphilis; he must putrefy, die in a filthy manner. He is despised by his neighbors, mocked, no longer greeted; they spit in front of him. There are allusions in the newspapers; the sermon is aimed at him; his sins are publicly made known."[8]

Kraepelin was not exaggerating. I see such patients today, but they are less common than they used to be, partly because they are treated earlier. For some years there was confusion over whether they were schizophrenic. The issue is complex but important. Sometimes the distinction between the two is very difficult to make. Mood congruence is one of the distinguishing features of a nonschizophrenic depressive psychosis. But it is important to make the distinction for our weapons against depression are powerful and the outlook for it much better than for schizophrenic illness.

One curious twist of depressive illness is its occasional tendency to show up as *chronic pain.*[9] More than once I have observed and treated such patients. Many are highly conscientious workers taking pride in what they do when from nowhere comes crippling pain in a joint for which no X ray or other special investigations can account. Blumer describes the patient's pain as continuous and patients as having a hypochondriacal fixation on the affected part. They are patients who deny emotional or interpersonal difficulties and idealize family relationships, and who not only have a history of relentless activity and of excessive work habits before the pain started, but who also continue to push themselves to work in spite of their pain, only giving in after they have successfully completed their objective.

One sixty-seven-year-old man was sent to me from the special pain clinic in the Health Sciences Centre in Winnipeg. For several years he had been crippled by low back pain for which no physical basis could be found. His pain had become much worse since his retirement and kept him more or less housebound. No treatments from conventional medicine nor from chiropractors had relieved it. He was depressed, but it was hard to know whether the depression resulted from his pain and the useless life he led following his retirement (which was his own view), or whether the pain and uselessness were caused by the depression. We faced a chicken-and-egg problem.

Since we had nothing to lose, he agreed to take a course of tricyclic antidepressants. ("I don't believe in pills, Doctor. Anyway, it's not in my head but in my back. But if you say I have to take pills. . . .") Six weeks later his youth and vigor had returned, his pain had gone, and he was busy doing repairs on his house and looking after his garden. It is only a pity that the treatment had not been started several years before.

Emotions That Mask Depression

Bipolar illness can also be mistaken for emotional instability. A study by Rifkin and his colleagues in Hillside Hospital, Glen Oaks, New York,[10] on a group of adolescents and of men and women in their twenties examined the effect of lithium on their behavior. The young people were constantly in trouble for unacceptable behavior and experienced mood swings in which they might appear happy (flirtatious, laughing, playing pranks) but during which they described themselves as more restless and driven than happy, alternating with periods of dejection. In the high periods they would defy authority, evade work and be manipulative. Their mood swings would last from hours to days. Their condition was named "emotionally unstable character disorder" by Rifkin. With lithium carbonate the moods evened out and the unstable behavior significantly improved.

Menopause and menstruation are in another group of conditions in which depression may be found and not at first seen for what it is. Women suffering premenstrual depression tended to be depression-free when placed on the pill even though symptoms such as headaches and swelling were not alleviated. Women who had no premenstrual depression became irritable and depressed when placed on the pill.[11]

Our understanding of the emotional illnesses surrounding female reproductive function is far from complete. The "three-day blues" many women experience following childbirth occasionally lasts longer than three days and can assume psychotic proportions. Of the psychoses following childbirth, the commonest is depression, but ideas about its origin vary.[12] Emotional breakdown following childbirth, commonly called *puerperal* or *postpartum* breakdown or depression has become a subject of more careful study in those countries where the law permits abortion when the pregnancy threatens not only the life of the mother but her health as well. In these areas psychiatrists are called on to predict the likelihood of mental illness where pregnancy occurs.

Sim in 1963[13] claimed that trivial "blues" occurred in 80% of deliveries but that serious depression occurred in only 1 parturition in 500. A much more careful prospective study by Pitt published five years later examined 305 women as they went through pregnancy and childbirth.[14] Pitt found that most of the women experienced a mild improvement in mood during the days following the birth but that 10.8%

developed "a true clinical depression" during the succeeding months. A typical mother would display symptoms such as worry about the child's feelings, guilt about her lack of feeling for the baby, inability to cope with the responsibility and resentment toward her husband. The women were distinguishable from others by a typical pattern on the MMPI psychological test. They were responsive to treatment, but not all depressed mothers wanted treatment, and some depressions were still unchanged two years after the birth of the child. The study raises ethical as well as technical problems. I personally have never recommended an abortion on the grounds of danger to the mother's mental health. In some cases I have had every reason to believe childbirth would probably be followed by mental illness. Why then my reluctance?

Quite apart from ethical considerations I have two reasons. First, depression (sometimes suicidal) often follows abortion itself. The decision to abort thus becomes a decision to gamble one grave uncertainty against another. Second, postpartum depressions can be treated and treated fairly easily. The psychological health of the mother is usually only in temporary jeopardy. I get the feeling when patients are referred to me for my opinion about the psychiatric dangers of a pregnancy that I am being asked to soothe the consciences of my medical colleagues who are themselves in doubt about the rightness of a particular abortion.

Early studies also seemed to suggest that hysterectomy was associated with an increased risk of depressive illness; indeed, that it might be the cause of the illness. Re-examination of older studies and the results of newer studies seem to suggest that the depressions are associated with menopause rather than with hysterectomy. Among women receiving hysterectomies are a disproportionate number of menopausal women. Among women attending an outpatient gynecology clinic for the first time about 10% were judged psychiatrically unwell and about half of these were menopausal.[15]

There seems to be a stronger case for the argument that depression leads to hysterectomy than that hysterectomy causes depression. In a more recent study Bellinger[16] carried out a prospective study by screening referrals to a gynecology clinic for psychiatric symptoms. She found them largely among menopausal women and particularly in those with previous contacts with psychiatry, particularly for depression, which suggests that menopausal depression may be the egg and hysterectomy the chicken.

Tragically, depression can be missed in older people and be mistaken for the confusion of senility. For a variety of reasons associated with degenerative changes in the brain, older patients grow forgetful and are at times incapable of caring for themselves. Their memories of past events may be sharp while those of more recent events may be very poor. Diagnoses such as "chronic brain syndrome" or "cerebral arteriosclerosis" accompany such patients as they are transferred to nursing homes.

But among the confused elderly are some people who are confused because they suffer from depressive illness. The poor memory has a very different explanation from senility and can be treated to restore a clear mind. Four cases are described in a recent article.[17] I myself have recently treated three elderly female patients, all of whom were confused and suffering from poor memories. Because of their poor physical shape they were given electroconvulsive therapy (ECT) rather than antidepressant medication. ECT is sometimes avoided because of its tendency to cause temporary deterioration of memory. In three of my own patients it restored their memories and replaced confusion with clarity and sharpness of mind.

In summary, depression wears many masks. It may come disguised by phobias, obsessions, compulsions or the need to consult a gynecologist. It may be mistaken for three-day baby blues or be colored by psychotic delusions. It may wear the mask of senility or confusion. But if care is taken to inquire methodically into all the patient's symptoms the disease may be unmasked.

The DSM III (*Diagnostic and Statistical Manual III*), already mentioned in chapter three, gives the following list of core symptoms of depressions.

A. Dysphoric mood [roughly, unpleasant or disagreeable] or loss of interest or pleasure in all or almost all usual activities and pastimes. The dysphoric mood is characterized by symptoms such as the following: depressed, sad, blue, hopeless, low, down in the dumps, irritable. The mood disturbance must be prominent and relatively persistent, but not necessarily the most dominant symptom, and does not include momentary shifts from one dysphoric mood to another dysphoric mood; e.g., anxiety to depression to anger, such are seen in states of acute psychotic turmoil. (For children under six, dysphoric mood may have to be inferred from a persistently sad facial expression.)

B. At least four of the following symptoms have each been present nearly every day for a period of at least two weeks (in children under six, at least three of the four).

  (1) poor appetite or significant weight loss (when not dieting) or increased appetite or significant weight gain (in children under six, consider failure to make expected weight gains);

  (2) insomnia or hypersomnia;

  (3) psychomotor agitation or retardation (but not merely subjective feelings of restlessness or being slowed down) (in children under six, hypoactivity);

  (4) loss of interest or pleasure in usual activities, or decrease in sexual drive not limited to a period when delusional or hallucinating (in children under six, signs of apathy);

  (5) loss of energy, fatigue;

  (6) feelings of worthlessness, self-reproach, or excessive

or inappropriate guilt (either may be delusional);

(7) complaints or evidence of diminished ability to think or concentrate, such as slowed thinking, or indecisiveness not associated with marked loosening of associations or incoherence;

(8) recurrent thoughts of death, suicidal ideation, wishes to be dead, or suicide attempt.[18]

These symptoms call for help. They call for medical help as well as for understanding, compassion and reassurance.

The Mania of Bipolar Illness

I'll not change life with any king
I ravisht am: can the world bring
More joy than still to laugh and smile
In pleasant toys time to beguile?
Do not, O do not trouble me,
So sweet content I feel and see
    All my joys to this are folly
    None so divine as melancholy.

Physicians and psychiatrists who write entertainingly are rare. Among the literary treasures of medicine is Robert Burton's seventeenth-century *The Anatomy of Melancholy*. Aurelianus was not alone in perceiving that depression had two sides. Robert Burton saw both sides and described accurately and entertainingly not only the darkness of despair but also the intoxication of the mania of what we now call bipolar affective illness.

I have referred several times to bipolar illness, a condition in which the patient experiences highs as well as lows or manic episodes as well as depressions. The illness differs from other depressive illnesses in a number of ways. First, and most obviously, the bouts of elation and excitement distinguish it. The effects of lithium on the illness also distinguish it. Lithium carbonate not only controls the highs but may also cut out or at least reduce the length and severity of the depressed periods. Lithium seems to affect cell membranes in bipolar patients in a different manner from the way it does in patients with a unipolar illness. In 1979 Ramsey and his coworkers gave lithium to a number of patients both bipolar and unipolar, as well as to a control group of seven healthy men.[19]

The membrane surrounding all types of body cells is basically similar and the transportation of ions (electrically charged atoms) across the membrane has a similar mechanism. Because it is difficult to observe what happens to lithium at the membrane surrounding nerve cells, Ramsey and his colleagues collected blood from their subjects. Blood, you will remember, consists of fluid plasma filled with millions of red cells called erythrocytes, which impart a red color to blood. Having collected whole blood (plasma and red cells), they compared the concentration of lithium in the plasma to the concentration inside the red cells. They found the ratio of the two measurements (the concentration in red cells to the concentration in the plasma) was much higher in patients with bipolar illness than in patients with unipolar illness and in normal controls. It appears that the properties of cell membranes (whether surrounding red cells or nerve cells) in bipolar patients have a different permeability to lithium. The fact seems to explain why some depressed patients can be helped with lithium and others not.

Bipolar illness also differs from unipolar illnesses in the way it is passed on from one generation to another. Most of the evidence suggests that it is transmitted by a dominant gene.[20] Interestingly it can also be identified in several generations of some bipolar patients by what is called a marker gene, a gene located close to the gene for bipolar illness and on the same chromosome. A number of studies have discovered a marker gene in some "bipolar families." It is a gene located on an X chromosome producing color blindness in the red/green spectrum. Its manifestation has been traced through several generations of certain families with a high incidence of bipolar illness.[21]

There is thus strong evidence that bipolar illness is a different condition from any of the unipolar varieties. Not only the manic symptoms distinguish it; so do the response to lithium, the mode of genetic transmission and differences in the properties of cell membranes.

Bipolar illness, however, may begin with a depression. It is therefore of great importance when one examines a depressed patient to ask about highs, times of excessive spending or excitement, and to ask about signs of bipolar illness in other family members. In a couple of instances I have treated patients who had no knowledge of their family history and claimed never to have been high through three depressions only to be surprised by a subsequent manic episode. For years I had regarded them as suffering from a unipolar illness.

The highs or manic periods vary in their intensity, some being so mild as to escape notice by anyone other than close friends and family members, others more noticeable because of the degree of excitement (what used to be called hypomania) and yet others so severe as to represent full-blown manic excitement.

Manic patients talk. At times they may be able to control the flow of words but at other times they talk animatedly and eagerly, words pouring from them in an unending stream, often seeming to sparkle with witticisms and puns. Yet the sparkle lies in the patient's enthusiasm rather than the brilliance of the utterance. Manic patients jump from topic to topic, but so amusingly that their friends may get caught in the excitement. Yet if their flow of talk is observed in a more detached way, it will become evident that their speech is a *flight of ideas*, an excessive switching from one idea to another. Often they are euphoric, but in a flash their joy may turn to rage if their wishes are opposed or their ideas challenged.

Their judgment is usually impaired. They embark on spending sprees, borrow money and invest it recklessly, make grandiose plans to accomplish impossible feats and seem endowed with endless energy. They sleep little yet need no rest. They stick their noses into other people's business, quarrel fiercely with former friends and move through their environment leaving a trail of disaster behind them.

They may drink excessively, flirt outrageously and move from affair to affair with sublime indifference to the consequences. If they are Christians their consciences seem to smile with approval on actions which normally would horrify them. God may tell them to change world history. They create uproars in bars, in churches and in social gatherings. They make long-distance telephone calls, unconcerned about time and money, and may run up bills in hotels and restaurants. Most remarkable of all is the pace they keep up as they flit from disaster to disaster.

If the nature of their illness is not discovered and treated it usually ends spontaneously, though its duration may vary from a few days to a couple of years. Happily they frequently get into trouble with the law so that police and court officials quickly refer them to psychiatric care.

If the manic phase runs its full course, the disorganization in speech and behavior can eventually become so pronounced that a professional, seeing the manic patient for the first time, may find diagnosis very difficult and may mistakenly assume the patient suffers from some form of schizophrenic excitement. Drs. Carlson and Goodwin were able a few years ago to review the records of 20 manic patients on whom very detailed records were kept and described three phases of the manic attack.[22]

In Stage I one patient was described as "a little pressured in speech, somewhat tangential [inclined to wander off the topic], hyperactive and happy." Another patient was "talking and laughing more, more irritable, seductive, said she was having ideas that might get her into trouble." A third patient was described as "distractable, complaining of racing thoughts, joking, intrusive, happy, unable to concentrate, impulsive, hyperverbal and singing."

In Stage II there were descriptions of more severely disorganized behavior. One patient was described as "pacing, manipulative, religious." He said he could not trust people. He was "crude, hypersexual, assaultive," and that he wanted to be King Kong. He "grimaced and postured as if in anguish." A female patient in Stage II took a bath wearing her nightgown, all the time yelling, crying, throwing anything within reach and threatening everyone. Another patient was described as hypersexual, hyperverbal, hyperactive, suspicious, angry, obscene, banging a urinal on the door and wanting to use the phone to buy stocks.

In Stage III patients maintained their extreme activity and talkativeness but became much more delusional and bizarre in their talk. They also lost track of where they were and of time. They were confused—delirious. As the manic episode subsided, patients moved back through Stage II to Stage I to normality.

One of my bipolar patients, normally a quiet, reserved and timid store clerk of twenty-five, was brought to me by the police after failing to pay for five cars he had bought. He had put his house up for sale, signed a contract on a much more expensive home ("Why should I live in a stinking little hole?") and set out to create a taxi company in a neighboring town, buying secondhand cars at outrageous prices, and succeeding in negotiating large bank loans. He was finally picked up by the police, walking down the main street throwing dollar bills over his shoulder as "a publicity stunt to get the taxi service started. In any case if you love people why not give them money? What's money for if not to let people have a good time?"

While not all patients reach Stage III, those who do become

more or less incoherent, uttering a series of unconnected words that make no sense while they remain excited and paranoid. Happily, most respond to lithium carbonate. But they do not seem anxious to take medication offered, mostly because they prefer the euphoria of mania to the banality of ordinary life.

Yet the consequences of the high can be devastating. More than one patient of mine has rushed into marriage during their manic episodes to persons with whom they have little or nothing in common, but whom they swept off their feet by their contagious enthusiasm. The subsequent marital trauma was pitiful to witness.

A California woman subject to manic attacks discontinued her lithium and slowly developed grandiose delusions that she was Jewish (she was Roman Catholic) and that she was a CIA agent involved in smashing an international spy ring. She kidnapped her two small children who were in the custody of her ex-husband and set out in her small car to reach Canada. Because she had no money, she paid for petrol, lodgings and meals by picking up male hitchhikers and giving them sexual favors. She was finally taken into custody by the police after creating an uproar in a Winnipeg bar. Her children were taken over by Children's Aid and attempts were made to locate their father as well as their mother's relatives and friends. While confined in a closed psychiatric ward she got in touch with Canadian immigration authorities and asked for political asylum. Her behavior alternated between open seductiveness and imperious rage.

Back on her lithium the personality that emerged was that of a courteous, gentle and sensible woman who was horrified by what she had done and dismayed that she had let herself become so psychotic. Her one desire was to return home and to see that her children were returned to the custody of her husband where she would have regular access to them.

The high of mania may also be a prelude to a profound depression. One of my patients who is unable to tolerate lithium regularly plunges into the depths of despair. Three weeks ago I recorded, "Is feeling 'wonderful.' Came into the office beautifully dressed, made up rather lavishly and with a special hair-do.... I suspect a plunge into depression is on the way."

There was nothing I could do to prevent it, except to warn the family and see her more frequently. To have given her antidepressants in anticipation of what was to come would have sent her higher yet. So now she is "very, very low" and fighting her way up with the help of antidepressant medication.

One consolation is that the number of patients with bipolar illness is much smaller than those who suffer depression alone. Happily too, we have more ability to combat these disorders than ever before.

But it is time that we looked at the causes of depression and elation. And since views vary widely, we will examine the commonest explanations in the next two chapters.

Part III
Understanding Depression & Suicide

6
Theories about Depression

Let not one bring learning, another
diligence, another religion, but everyone
bring all; and as many ingredients enter
into a receipt [prescription], so may
many men make the receipt.
John Donne, Meditations 1624

I mentioned earlier that rival schools entertain rival views about the causes and the nature of depression. I also mentioned that in many universities there is a new and healthy tendency for interdisciplinary studies and for serious attempts to re-evaluate the place of different views. To my mind two articles by Akiskal and McKinney constitute a landmark in our attempts to overcome the isolation and hostility of rival schools, and to subject all views to impartial scrutiny and wide-scale investigation.[1]

Akiskal and McKinney took a careful look at ten of the most popular models of depression; that is, at ten common ways the condition is looked at and explained by different theorists.

More than this, they looked at the possibility that depression might be a final common pathway, a condition which has a common set of recognizable signs and symptoms but which may represent a diverse group of illnesses that have different causes but ultimately behave the same.

But first let us look at ten competing models of depression grouped under five headings, and at evidence supporting some of them. I have adapted them below from Akiskal and McKinney.[2]

Psychoanalytical School
Model 1. Aggression turned inward.
Model 2. Object loss.
Model 3. Loss of self-esteem.
Model 4. Negative cognitive set.
Behavioral School
Model 5. Learned helplessness.
Model 6. Loss of reinforcement.
Sociological School
Model 7. Loss of role status.
Existential School
Model 8. Loss of meaning of existence.
Biological School
Model 9. Impairment of biogenic amine.
Model 10. Neurophysiological malfunction.

The list may look formidable to you if you have no background in the human sciences. Let me try to explain some of the terms. And as I do so, let us also look at some of the causes of depression.

Model 1: Aggression Turned Inward (Psychoanalytical School)

Psychoanalysis is a broad movement that includes widely differing theories. Common to all of them are ideas first propounded by Sigmund Freud. According to Freud, our minds are energy systems. Different mental areas (such as conscious and unconscious, id, ego and superego) harbor processes that are in tension with one another. Our conscious words, thoughts and actions are influenced more than we realize by these tensions and by motivations we are not always aware of.

The first psychoanalytic views, indeed the first psychiatric attempts in modern times, to explain depression were propounded by Karl Abraham[3] and Sigmund Freud. To Abraham and Freud depression consisted of anger against oneself, anger which might more logically be expressed against someone else, but which instead was turned inward and for that reason called retroflexed rage. In his 1916 paper "Mourning and Melancholia" Freud tried to distinguish the sadness or the grief we all experience over bereavement from what he called *melancholia,* a term which means roughly the same as the term *primary depression* I mentioned before.

"The distinguishing features of melancholia," Freud stated, "are a profoundly painful dejection, abrogation of interest in the outside world, loss of the capacity to love, inhibition of all activity, and a lowering of the self-regarding feelings to a degree that finds utterance in self-reproaches and self-revilings, and culminates in a delusional expectation of punishment."[4]

Melancholia, Freud thought, had a more complex explanation than normal grief. A bereaved and melancholic boy would feel anger toward the father who had "abandoned" him. But since rage against the dead would be shocking to the superego, he would *identify* with his father and *introject* him, taking his father "inside" himself so that his father became a part of his own psyche. The process would take place without the boy's awareness but would account for the inwardly directed rage. Freud noted that many melancholics tended to blame and even to heap abuse on themselves. Among legitimate self-reproaches he would discover quite unrealistic ones which he felt were really being directed at the lost person. "The woman who loudly pities her husband for being bound to such a poor creature as herself is really accusing her husband of being a poor creature in some sense or other."[5]

I have oversimplified Freudian theory, but it is interesting to note that Freud felt that more than a psychological explanation was involved. He noted the experience of some depressed people who spoke of a lightening or an alleviation of their mood in the evening, constituting what we now call a diurnal mood variation. This he attributed to "a somatic factor . . . [and is] not explicable psychologically." He speculated, in fact, that part of the depression may be "directly due to toxins . . . in certain forms of the disease."[6] Unfortunately, psychoanalysts for many years ignored Freud's suggestions about the physical aspects of melancholia.

Abraham was not only a theorist but an astute clinical observer. His theory on melancholia was much like Freud's; indeed, Freud quoted Abraham in "Mourning and Melancholia."[7] Abraham, however, made an important observation which analysts and nonanalysts too often ignore, that childhood bereavement left scars. Children bereaved of parents became vulnerable to melancholia in later life and suffered from what Abraham called primal parathymia.[8] Later we will look more closely at the matter of vulnerability to depression and its relationship to childhood bereavement.

I have spent time on the retroflexed-rage view of depression because it remains a widely believed popular myth. Akiskal and McKinney comment, "Even though this is the most widely quoted psychological conceptualization of depression, there is little systematic evidence to substantiate it."[9] There may be some truth to the theory that not only are Freud's ideas difficult to prove, but they also serve no valuable purpose. We cannot make people better by applying it. Those depressed people who are not already hostile do not get better when they are encouraged to direct their rage outwardly. Sometimes, as Akiskal and McKinney point out, our attempts in this direction have "disastrous consequences."

But I must qualify my statement. While anger-against-the-self does not account for serious depressive illness, it certainly does account for the depressed mood some of us feel at times.

If we need certain people's approval or love, we may find it hard to be angry with them, simply because we fear their loss of approval. We want them to go on loving us. Without realizing what we are doing, we turn our anger on ourselves. We begin in our despondency to blame ourselves for whatever may have happened. It is easier to blame ourselves than the person whose approval we need. But such retroflexed rage does not represent an illness so much as a discouraged mood that can be helped by counseling and psychotherapy.

Model 2: Object Loss (Psychoanalytical School)

To psychoanalysts the term *object* has a technical meaning. It denotes any person or thing with which the subject is emotionally involved. Thus *object loss* may refer to the death of a parent, loss of one's home or the like. Abraham, in talking about primal parathymia, was speaking of the long-term results of parent loss—technically the loss of an object. What do we know about the bereavement of infants?

Of the many attacks on classical psychoanalytic theory, few have been more interesting or have contributed more significantly to analytic theory than Harry Harlow's monkey experiments. Early analytic theory, in stressing the importance of mother-love in infants, had focused attention on the mother's breasts. They theorized that the contact of the baby's lips with the maternal breast was critical in reassuring the child it was loved. The child's emotional development depended on satisfactory nursing, satisfactory not merely in its mechanical efficiency but in meeting the infant's powerful oral cravings.

Harlow's experiments demonstrated clearly that whatever might be the case for human infants, breasts were of little importance in the emotional development of infant macaque monkeys.[10] Harlow and his wife conducted a series of experiments ingeniously contrived to discover what constitutes "being loved" to a baby monkey. "We discovered," Harlow wrote, " . . . that a baby monkey raised on a bare wire-mesh cage floor survives with difficulty, if at all, during the first five days of life. If a wire mesh cone is introduced the baby does better, and if the cone is covered with terry cloth, husky, healthy, happy babies evolve." Love, Harlow began to think, meant "contact comfort," the feeling of something soft and supportive beneath one's body.

He began to construct surrogate mothers (mechanical mother substitutes) made of wire mesh. Some of the "mothers" had a covering of terry cloth to impart a soft feeling. Feeding bottles served as substitutes for breasts. In some cages, for instance, Harlow would have two "mothers," one a wire mesh cone with a crude replica of a macaque monkey's face above it, an electric bulb beneath the cone to provide gentle warmth and a feeding bottle from whose nipple the infant could nurse. In the same cage there could be another "mother," identical with the first having an electric bulb for warmth but lacking a "breast" and covered with terry toweling. "The result," Harlow comments about the second mother, "was a mother, soft, warm and tender, a mother with infinite patience, a mother available twenty-four hours a day, a mother that never scolded her infant and never struck or bit her baby in anger."

The arrangement varied from cage to cage and experiment to experiment. Sometimes the soft, warm mother would also have a "breast," so that there were two feeding sources. But whatever the arrangement, it quickly became plain that the terry-covered mother was the source of emotional comfort to the infant who would spend a disproportionate amount of time with her. If she lacked a "breast" the infant would remain with the wire mother only long enough to nurse. When it was done feeding, it would return to the terry-cloth mother. Or if it was playing away from both mothers and was startled by a loud noise, invariably it would flee for security to the terry-cloth mother.

Denied a terry-cloth mother and provided only with a wire-mesh mother, it would often fail to thrive, would become restless, easily frightened, and might die.

Many years before the Harlow experiments René Spitz, a psychoanalyst, had become intrigued by what he called anaclitic depression in infants reared in orphanages. About 15% of infants in orphanages failed to thrive, became restless, apathetic and apprehensive, crying feebly. They withdrew, were retarded in their development, would not respond to stimuli, be slow of movement, look dejected and become stuporous. Slowly they would cease to nurse, would lose weight and eventually die.[11]

Spitz discovered that if from among the staff of the orphanage he could find someone who could establish contact with the infant and continue to spend time exclusively with the infant, picking it up, encouraging it to nurse, talking to it, the depression would reverse and the baby would recover. The findings of Harlow and of Spitz seem to suggest two things. First, mother-infant contact was vital to the well-being and even to the life of infants; and second, the contact involved much more than the sensation of sucking; in fact, sucking was relatively unimportant.

The Harlow experiments revealed something else. Where a group of infant monkeys were taken from their real mothers and confined in a cage with a terry-cloth mother, their development would be normal—until the terry-cloth mother was taken away. At that point, instead of clinging to a terry-cloth mother, the infants would spend long periods clinging closely to one another. Provided they continued to have one another to cling to, all would eventually go well. But if they were separated, the same picture of failing to thrive and of death would supervene. "One can conclude," write Akiskal and McKinney, "that the disruption of an attachment bond, whether infant-mother, or infant-infant, is a powerful inducer of psychopathology of the 'depressive' type."[12]

Breaking the Bonds of Love

During the past twenty-five years a great deal has been written about attachment bonds (which we might call the bonds of love) and the disastrous effects of their disruption, which include depression. As the Harlows and others began to discover, the "disruption of attachment bonds" did not only prove disastrous at the time, but also opened the way for later problems. Psychoanalysts may not have been accurate about exactly what in early life sowed trouble for later development, but they were right in supposing that infantile experiences had critical importance for the future. Abraham was right. Childhood bereavement left many individuals vulnerable to later depression.

The first person to elaborate a comprehensive theory about attachment was Dr. John Bowlby, a psychiatrist who has been linked for many years with the Tavistock Clinic in London.[13] Bowlby combined the observations of ethologists (biologists who study animals in their natural habitat) with psychoanalysis and other insights. As early as 1952, along with a fellow worker, he had noted three phases in an infant's reaction to separation from its mother.[14] There was a *protest phase* in which the child would display restlessness and tearfulness, a *despair phase* of apathy and withdrawal, and a *detachment phase* during which the infant would reject the mother when contact was renewed. Bowlby has written extensively on bonding. A recent and lucid article is entitled, "The Making and Breaking of Affectional Bonds."[15]

Bonding or *attachment* refers to our human capacity to make strong bonds of love with other human beings, whether parents, children, friends, lovers or spouses. It is the process by which emotional ties are formed. When we use phrases such as "The baby means everything to her" or "The two of them are very close," we are talking about affectional bonding. We need not concern ourselves here with how the bonds are formed, nor with the formative roles of physical contact, sight, smell and hearing. From the viewpoint of depression we are more concerned with what happens when the bonds are torn apart and with the psychic wounds the disruption causes, both immediately and over the course of years.

Among the immediate effects are anxiety, anger, depression and detachment. In addition the development of personality can be profoundly affected by prematurely ruptured attachments, one of the long-term results being increased vulnerability to depressive illness.

A number of studies in Scotland link some depression in adult women with the loss of a parent before their tenth year[16] and a recent re-evaluation of all the literature about the role of bereavement and loss in childhood concludes that such events do leave us vulnerable to later depressive illness.[17]

Two recent London studies have confirmed and elaborated the findings. In the different groups of women studied, the vulnerability to depression was found to be associated with:

1) the loss of a mother before the age of eleven;
2) the presence at home of three or more children under fourteen;
3) the lack of a confiding relationship with a husband; and
4) the lack of full-time or part-time employment outside the home.[18]

The same study seeks to clarify further the precise relationship between early bereavement and subsequent depression. To lose one's father or brothers or sisters before age seventeen did not seem to give rise to depression in later life; neither did the loss of a mother when the subject was between eleven and seventeen prove significant. But the loss of a mother before eleven did seem to predispose one to depression in later life. To lose one's mother through death meant that the depression could reach psychotic proportions.

There are now many studies linking depression in adult life with childhood bereavement. In one study 216 depressed patients were compared with two groups of nondepressed people of similar age and circumstances. Of the depressed patients studied, 41% had suffered bereavement as children, whereas in the two control groups the bereavement had occurred respectively in 16% and in 12%. Thus childhood bereavement does not necessarily produce depression in adulthood nor is all adult depression the result of childhood bereavement. But bereavement can be a powerful influence.[19]

When the statistics in this particular study were examined more closely a direct relationship was found between the age at which bereavement occurred and the number of patients who succumbed to depression. Most of the depressed patients experienced bereavement during the first four years of life, a smaller number between the ages of five and nine, and the smallest number between ten and fourteen.

All of us pass through a period of grief and mourning when we are bereaved. The process is normal and calls for no treatment. It usually lasts only two or three months provided we are in normal health and enjoy the support of family and friends. It is only when mourning becomes incapacitating and unduly prolonged that we should be alert to the fact that we are no longer dealing with the normal but with disease. The special vulnerability may have arisen from childhood bereavement, or it may have other explanations. But clearly some of us face the possibility of depressive illness.

One investigator studied the histories of 3,245 psychiatric patients with many different diagnoses and discovered that those whose illness had begun within six months of the death of a parent, spouse, sibling or child were all people at high risk for affective (depressive) illness. For them, bereavement was the precipitating cause of an illness to which they were already vulnerable.[20] Bereavement, in fact, was shown as long ago as 1958 to precipitate not only depressive illness but a variety of physical ailments.[21]

Slowly the evidence has become overwhelming. By whatever name we refer to it (object loss, disruption of affectional bonds), the loss in early childhood of a parent makes us susceptible to later depressive illness. It is not *the* cause of depressive illness. Depressive illness will not necessarily follow it. But it is one predisposing cause which contributes in many people to depression in later life.

Model 3: Loss of Self-esteem (Psychoanalytical School)

So far we have looked at two models of depression arising among psychoanalytical theorists, one of which (retroflexed rage) has little evidence to support it and the other of which (object loss) has a great deal to support it.

The third model is provided by Bibring. Early psychoanalysis concentrated on what we now call id psychology, a focus on unconscious and instinctual drives. More recent thinking has broken away from id psychology to focus on what are called ego states. An ego state is a condition arising from the way one handles reality. Bibring was perhaps the first analytic thinker to see depression as an ego state, divorced from aggressive drives. He suggested that helplessness was the critical factor in depression, helplessness to achieve one's goals. To express the matter in analytic terms, the ego (the conscious, decision-making part of us) suffers a narcissistic injury and collapses when it perceives that its ideals (ego ideals) are unattainable. An ego ideal might be anything, a wish to be loved or to be "good" (holy) or to be secure or strong or kind or whatever.[22]

In simple terms we lose self-esteem when we fail to meet our own view of what is good and right. We are discouraged on perceiving the appalling gap between what we want to be and what we are, between our goals and our ability to perform. Christians will readily understand the dilemma. "Oh, wretched persons that we are! Who shall deliver us from this body of death?"

Bibring, however, would offer a different solution from Paul's. And his focus is different. The central dilemma to

Bibring is not that failing to achieve our goals is distressing, but that it lies at the core of serious depression. Is he correct? Certainly many depressed people lament their helplessness. Indeed, one of the most frustrating features of real depression is the victim's inability to do anything.

Yet Bibring presents us with what may be a chicken-and-egg problem. Though many depressed people are aware of the gap between their goals and their capacity to achieve them, the question remains: Is the gap the cause of their depression or is it a result? Has depression distorted the picture so that the victim cannot perform even simple tasks?

We know, for instance, that a grossly exaggerated sense of guilt is a feature of many depressions and that the sense of guilt is unrealistic and will disappear as the depression lifts. In this case the guilt is a correlate of the depression, something that comes and goes with it. We also know that attempts to deal with the sense of guilt are in most cases totally ineffective, and will not (unlike the example in the opening chapter of this book) do anything to alleviate the depression. Is it possible that Bibring's helplessness is like the sense of guilt, something that merely accompanies depression, as blossoms accompany spring? The question is important. If helplessness is a correlate of sickness, we must treat the sickness. If sickness is the result of unreached goals, we should help people reach goals. I believe Bibring's view fails to get to the root of the problem. He describes not a cause but a symptom of depressive illness. I believe helplessness is just one of many results of depressive illness.

A month or so ago a young man was persuaded to see me who seemed to be suffering from a severe depression. He complained of weight loss, sleeplessness, tiredness, inability to concentrate and several other depressive symptoms which had been present for more than a year. He was convinced, however, that the problem was purely spiritual. "I know I should be outgoing and relate warmly to people, but I constantly fail," he told me. "I don't love others. I only love my-self. I am defeated constantly." He accepted the possibility that his state of mind might arise from a physical illness and that a trial of antidepressant medication might be of value. But he requested time to think about the matter. In the end he refused medication, certain that his problem was spiritual. The Bible school he was attending, however, refused to allow him to continue his studies unless he accepted my treatment. Reluctantly he agreed and was amazed two months later at his increased ability to concentrate, his greater energy and a growing ability to reach out to others. In his case, helplessness was clearly a depressive symptom.

Model 4: Negative Cognitive Set (Psychoanalytical School)

A more serious case has for many years been made by Aaron T. Beck and by Albert Ellis[23] for hopelessness as the root of depression. Beck is a champion of what is known as a cognitive set view of depression. Beck's view of depression, like Bibring's, is a radical departure from id psychology and emphasizes cognition (conscious thought). It may for this reason be appealing to many Christians. Beck's views have been widely circulated via numerous articles and by his textbook on depression.[24]

They are interesting not only because he provides experimental data to support them but also because they find support in animal behavioral experiments. In recent articles Beck's views are updated and clarified.[25] Depression consists of "an altered style of cognition" (roughly, unusual habits of thinking) with a "cognitive triad" consisting of:

1. a negative view of oneself;
2. negative interpretations of one's experiences; and
3. a negative view of the future.

The triad is associated with hopelessness which is for Beck the key to depression, just as helplessness was the key to Bibring. Thus we might suggest the same criticism of Beck as of

Bibring and ask whether negative views of oneself, one's experiences and of the future are results of rather than causes of depression.

Beck and his colleagues, however, have made vigorous attempts to change the "cognitive style" of depressed patients in psychotherapy. If the cognitive triad is merely a correlate of depression, it is hard to see how depression will lift when the triad is changed by psychotherapy. And this is precisely what Beck and his coworkers claim.

Beck's views seem to have moderated a little over the years. In his early writings he seemed unwilling to consider the value of antidepressant medication. Now, while still claiming the superiority of cognitive therapy, he is more willing to concede that they have a place. In a 1977 study Rush (one of Beck's associates) compared short-term cognitive therapy with antidepressants in the treatment of 14 unipolar depressive patients who were randomly assigned to one treatment or the other over a period of twelve weeks. They claimed that while both chemical and psychotherapeutic treatments were "highly effective," the cognitive therapy was statistically superior.[26]

Beck's work must be taken seriously and will be discussed more fully in chapter ten on psychotherapies. Nevertheless, the evidence supporting his claims is as yet slender compared with the massive and overwhelming body of worldwide literature demonstrating the effectiveness of antidepressants. It is likely that the ideal will at some future date combine efforts at a cognitive as well as a chemical level. In the meantime very large trials involving a number of academic centers are testing the relative effectiveness of the two types of treatment.

One problem in assessing Rush's 1977 study is that of knowing both the severity of the depressions and the reliability of the measures of improvement. Most severe depressions are "unreachable" by psychotherapy. Beck and his coworkers have constructed rating scales (pp. 68-69) to assess the severity of depressions. Other rating scales (pp. 70-71), such as the Hamilton Scale, are designed to assess deeper depressions. It is possible that Rush's study included few of the very severe depressions with which some of us deal and that the results may reflect the effectiveness of cognitive therapy in a different population than those in many trials of antidepressants.

The so-called cognitive therapy used by Rush's team also includes behavioral components.[27] It is partly behavioral and partly ego-psychological treatment. I believe that while Beck puts his finger on a core symptom, and while (to return to chapter three) function may in turn affect the body, there are times when cognitive therapy will work well and other times when it will be an expensive waste of time.

Models 5-7: Sociological and Behavioral Schools

Behaviorism explains human behavior in terms of reinforcement (or reward) and aversive conditioning (or punishment). Its theorists do not concern themselves with intrapsychic processes (what goes on "in the mind") but with observable behavior and its antecedents. Behavior that is rewarded will be repeated. If you ever go to a circus, notice that every time an animal performs a trick, the trainer will pop something into its mouth or lavish extra affection on it. The animal's behavior has been shaped by rewarding those behaviors the trainer wants to elicit. Punishment is generally considered by behaviorists to be less efficient than reward, but it also has a place. Punishment to a behaviorist means an unpleasant experience immediately following a certain behavior.

I am vividly reminded of the shower in the bathtub of a house we used to live in. A small lever on the wall diverted the flow of water from the tap to the shower head. It was always my intention to let the water flow from the taps until it reached the right temperature before I turned on the shower. Several times in succession, however, I leaned over the tub and turned on the taps only to be shocked by a cold drenching on the back of my head and shoulders. Someone had left the little lever in the shower position. The result of my being "punished" for touching the taps was that I became nervous about turning them on at all. I would cringe instinctively as I leaned forward to grasp them. My previous experience of unpleasantly cold water on my back would arrest the motion of my hand. Even when I was sure that the lever was in the correct position I still had to force myself to turn the taps. My error had produced aversive conditioning, training me to avoid touching the taps.

Behavioral views and sociological views have much in common. If society rewards depressed behavior (sad looks, expressions of pain) by responding with sympathy, then the depressed behavior will be reinforced. (Some of us intuitively adopt a behaviorist model when we discuss a sulky child, "Take no notice of him. He'll get over it.")

But sociologists have other theories of depression which have more in common with ego psychologists. Becker [28] sees depression following the loss of symbolic possessions (power, prestige roles, identity and the like).

Perhaps the most interesting sociological observations come from Weissman and Klerman, who in 1977 reviewed 37 studies and surveys of depression[29] enquiring particularly why women suffer more depression than men.

Precise figures are not easy to determine, but some authorities suggest that women suffer twice as much depression as men. Among the many traditional suggestions is the idea that men turn to alcohol while women get depressed. Weissman and Klerman, in their painstaking analysis, conclude that the difference between male and female depression is real and not accounted for by some error in the method of research. They discuss genetics (which we will look at later), male alcoholism and endocrinology, concluding "that marriage has a protective effect for males but a detrimental effect for women. This supports the view that elements in the traditional female role may contribute to depression."

Reward and Punishment! "Go!" and "Stop!"

Before considering behavioral models further, we need to look first at the neurophysiology and neuroanatomy of depression. Elsewhere[30] I described experiments carried out in rats by James Olds.[31] While brain physiology is far more complex than Olds' work suggests and while we must be cautious about applying the results of animal experiments to humans, he does provide a model for understanding behavior. Olds discovered what initially was called a reward center in the brain of rats. He had inserted electrodes into a rat's brain and discovered by chance that when the electrode was stimulated (that is, when a tiny electrical current was released from the tip of the electrode), the rat seemed to experience great pleasure. By pressing a lever in its cage the rat could stimulate itself and would continue to do so until it fell down exhausted.

Olds killed the rat and discovered that the tip of the electrode was located in a region of the brain immediately in front of the hypothalamus, the septal or prefrontal area. Carefully placing electrodes in this area in the brains of more rats, he discovered that some of them would stimulate themselves as many as 3,000 times an hour until they too fell into an exhausted sleep.[32]

A little further back in the rat brain, in the posterior region of the hypothalamus, was a nerve center with very different properties from those of the prefrontal area. If the prefrontal (septal) area was a reward center, delighting the rat with the exquisite pleasure afforded by pressing the lever to stimulate itself, stimulation of electrodes placed further back produced a very different effect. To a rat such stimulation was exceedingly unpleasant, so unpleasant that it would avoid the lever. If Olds continued cruelly to stimulate the electrodes, the rat would refuse food, lose weight and eventually die. Stimulation of the "punishment area" of rat brains produced the equivalent of human depression.

If, however, two electrodes were present, one in the punishment center and the other in the reward center, stimulation of the reward center could reverse the process leading to depression and death, and substitute a process leading to joy and life.

Similar experiments, some of them unethical, have been carried out in human beings. Subjects stimulated in the "reward area" of their brains find it hard to describe the sensation they experience, but all agree that the experience is glorious and ecstatic. Stimulation in the punishment center, conversely, is indescribably unpleasant, awakening fear, horror and dismay. It would appear that the two systems counteract each other and that the balance of power between them determines our experience, whether of pleasure or of pain.

Nerve systems are roughly parallel to (but infinitely more complex than) electrical systems. Some psychologists refer to the pleasure system as the go system because its predominance seems to encourage action and problem solving. They refer to the punishment system as the stop system because its predominance induces inactivity. The two systems are so delicately balanced that in most of us the desire to act is tempered by an instinct to be careful and cautious.

Interestingly, each system operates by a different electrochemical mix. The go system is noradrenergic, dependent on the presence of noradrenaline (or norepinephrine) to work effectively. The stop system is called cholinergic, activated by a chemical called acetyl-choline.[33]

Learned Helplessness

Let us now turn to some very interesting experiments carried out by the behaviorist Seligman at the University of Pennsylvania. Seligman experimented with dogs. Picture if you will an enclosure divided into two parts by a barrier low enough for a dog to jump from one part of the enclosure to the other. The floor of one half of the enclosure is an electrical grid.

If a current is passed through the grid, a dog will leap over the barrier into the safe area. No matter how many times it is placed on the grid it will leap to safety and show no ill effects from the experiment. Seligman then placed some dogs in a harness so that they were unable to escape the shocks. Under these circumstances the dogs did show evidence of harm. They lost weight and became jittery, nervous and obviously sick. More importantly, when the harness was removed they made no attempt to leap over the barrier to escape the electric shocks administered through the grid. Instead they remained passive, pathetically enduring any shocks that came their way, growing thinner and sicker.[34]

To express the matter crudely and simply, the dogs had learned that it was futile to try to escape unpleasant experiences. There was nothing they could do. *They were helpless, hopeless.* Nevertheless, they could learn. When the experimenters persistently lifted them across the barrier into the "safe" area, the dogs would eventually learn that the shock could be avoided. With the new learning they would begin to jump the barrier unaided. Slowly they would gain weight, would lose their air of nervousness and hopelessness, and would become normal dogs again.[35]

Perhaps we are now in a position to fit some pieces of the jigsaw of depression into place. Let us suppose that the dogs had learned what Bibring referred to as helplessness and what Beck called hopelessness. In that case we can suggest that the "learning" can be viewed as a kind of tinkering with the electrochemical systems in the dogs' brains, resulting in a shift of the balance between reward and punishment centers, between stop and go systems. If so the condition of the "depressed" dogs might be changed either by fooling with the chemistry of their brains (so that the adrenergic system began to predominate over the cholinergic system) or by teaching them that they could escape from despair.

Some questions remain, for animal experiments do not always apply to human behavior. If human depression is viewed as *learned helplessness* or *learned hopelessness,* can human beings, like dogs, relearn? Can we learn to take active steps to overcome our despair? Beck and Bibring would both answer yes. My own guess would be in some cases yes but in others (more severe cases of depression) no. Happily, as we shall see later, a readjustment of the electrochemical balance of the central nervous system will restore patients to health and deliver human victims from the despair occasioned by an electrochemical imbalance in their brains.

There have been criticisms of Seligman's work. Vicky Riperre in a carefully reasoned article warned about the problems of applying animal models to human beings and asked whether dog depression is the same as human depression. In addition she makes theoretical criticisms of Seligman's behavioral model.[36] But Seligman's experiments are suggestive. Is there a parallel between humans and dogs in this instance? Can humans "learn" to get rid of depression by forcefully being shown solutions to their problems? As yet there is no clear consensus on their subject.

The issue of freedom and free will also raises its head. Are we the victims of body chemistry? Do we lose our freedom with an imbalance of adrenergic and cholinergic systems? All the theories I have mentioned are deterministic. There are elements of truth in most of them. How do we reconcile them with a biblical view of human nature?

Freedom cannot be described in absolute terms, but in degrees. Freedom is part of physical and spiritual health. It is also a result of the gospel. Conversely, we become less free the sicker we are, whether morally or physically. The more "mentally" sick we become, the more our freedom is impaired. To be restored to health is to be restored to a measure of freedom. Or expressed in the terms used earlier, impaired bodily health will mean impaired bodily function (mind). And impaired function may interfere with bodily freedom. People whose depression robs them of freedom must be helped by any ethical means we have available. If I can restore someone's physical freedom by mending a fractured femur, I see nothing wrong with restoring their volitional freedom by adjusting their disordered brain biochemistry. But more of this anon.

Before we leave the subject of brain physiology, we should note that more sophisticated investigations of the brain are available. Among these is P.E.T. (positron-electron tomography), a more advanced development of C.A.T. (computerized axial tomography). By the use of positron-labeled water, carbon dioxide, dopamine, norepinephrine and psychotropic drugs, three-dimensional images can be constructed to indicate the blood flow to various centers in the brain, as well as the metabolism of neurotransmitters (see next chapter) and psychotropic drugs. Already P.E.T. studies in schizophrenia and affective illnesses show promise of clarifying the brain metabolism of these illnesses.[37]

There remains the curious question of what are known as circadian rhythms in depression. Circadian rhythms arise from biological clocks in our brains that govern the timing of waking and sleeping and the preparation of the body through each hour of the twenty-four-hour cycle. Body metabolism does not take place at a constant rate but at rates varying with demands usually made on us at regular times. Our temperatures will vary as will the output of many body hormones. If depression is *merely* psychological, it is strange to find that in affective illness the biological clocks governing circadian rhythms are anywhere between one and three hours out of phase.[38]

Model 8: Loss of Meaning of Existence (Existential School)
Existentialists in general view anxiety and depression as the

result of life's meaninglessness. In a later chapter, on suicide, we shall glance briefly at Camus's famous comment in his essay on Sisyphus that suicide is the only philosophical problem. Christians are more familiar, however, with the writings of Victor Frankl. Frankl, a Jewish psychoanalyst, was a concentration-camp victim in World War 2. He tells the story in his book *Man's Search for Meaning.* Pondering the dilemma of why some of the prisoners flung themselves against electrified barbed wire, inviting a volley of machine-gun fire to signal their suicidal end, while others patiently endured, finding the will to live, he slowly formulated his theory of the human drive for meaning.

Frankl suggests that in addition to Freud's drive for love (eros), aggression and death (thanatos), there exists a human drive to find the meaning of existence. He quotes Nietzsche's dictum that men and women will endure any suffering or hardship if they understand the why of their existence. To Frankl himself a projected book on psychiatry supplied the why. He had to survive in order that he might complete his work and give his book to the world.

Frankl coined the term *noogenic neurosis,* which he saw as the neurosis of the postwar world—a widespread neurotic depression arising from the pointlessness and meaninglessness of life. Slowly he developed his system of logotherapy, an endeavor to search with each of his patients for the meaning of their personal existence, convinced that if they could discover the why of their lives, they would somehow find how to endure any pain or hardship.

Frankl is for Christians both a delight and a frustration. He is a delight in his grasp of the fundamental fact that we need to understand why we are alive. He is a frustration in that he eludes the basic question (the ultimate meaning of existence), confining himself to the idiosyncratic meaning of each person's existence. An abandoned mother, for example, can be helped to endure hardship by understanding that the meaning of her life consists in creating a future for her crippled child.

Without a doubt, Frankl's perspective and his reminder to the Christian that suffering is not meaningless are invaluable. Unquestionably, seriously depressed people can be helped if they can only grasp that their experience has purpose and significance. Yet there are some who cannot grasp this, whose physical brains are too sluggish to lift them from the foul mire of despair. Their distress must be alleviated in other ways. To understand why, we will need to dig more deeply into an understanding of the bodily nature of depression.

7
Fearfully & Wonderfully Made

For thou didst form my inward
parts,
  thou didst knit me together
    in my mother's womb.
I praise thee, for thou art fearful
and wonderful.
  Wonderful are thy works!
Thou knowest me right well;
  my frame was not hidden
    from thee,
when I was being made in secret,
  intricately wrought in the
    depths of the earth.
Psalm 139:13-15

The Cosmos is all darkness. It is
illuminated by the manifestation of
God in it. Whoever sees the Cosmos
and does not contemplate Him
in or by it or before it or after
it is in need of light and is veiled
from the sun of (understanding)
by the clouds of created things.
Ibn 'Ata' illah. The Book of
Wisdom 1:14

We looked in the previous chapter at the critical balance between the brain's go or pleasure system and its stop or pain system—each subject to chemical control—one adrenergic (controlled by noradrenaline or norepinephrine), the other cholinergic (operated by acetylcholine). We noted from Seligman's experiments with dogs that depression, even fatal depression, can be learned and that (in dogs at least) it can be unlearned by teaching a depressed dog that it can escape, that it need not remain helpless and hopeless.

Yet I hope that we have also seen that the neurochemical

balance of stop and go centers is not set once and for all to control our behavior throughout life. For instance, it is not independent of things going on around us. True, its function depends to some degree on things that happened before we were even conceived.[1] Certainly events in our early life (such as disrupted affectional bonds) may have affected its tendency to shift one way or another while there is some evidence that the balance may be modified by certain types of psychotherapy, behavior therapy and chemical tinkering. While we are healthy, we seem to be able to control it ourselves.

Models 9-10: Biological Schools

In this chapter we shall look simultaneously at the two biological models—at the impairment of biogenic amine (neurotransmitter) mechanisms and of the neurophysiology of brain cells. As we do so, let me stress the importance of realizing that changes in brain chemistry (on a molecular level) and neurophysiology (on a larger level) are what we call correlates of depressive illness, events which occur simultaneously with the illness but which are not necessarily their causes, even though we may cure patients by "normalizing" what is going on in the brain.

Let us then take a preliminary look at the human brain itself. We must approach it cautiously. Nothing on earth, indeed nothing that we know of in the universe, is so complex. From the scientist it calls for caution against leaping to conclusions. From the Christian it calls for worship to God whose creations are marvelous beyond description. From all of us it calls for respect. It must not be tampered with lightly. It was created with a purpose. It is that part of the human body which most gives rise not only to our humanity but also to our godlikeness.

The human brain has sometimes been (foolishly) compared with a computer. *Its every cell is a computer.* Each of its neurons

Figure 5
A Neuron

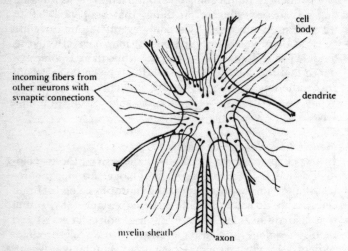

cell body

incoming fibers from other neurons with synaptic connections

dendrite

myelin sheath   axon

Adapted from D. Gareth Jones, Our Fragile Brains *(Leicester: Inter-Varsity Press, 1981), p. 39.*

(nerve cells which are the brain's building blocks) is a sort of electrochemical-factory-cum-microcomputer-cum-communication-system. It is a living, moving, breathing marvel. And in our brains there exist about one hundred billion of these living organisms—about as many as the number of stars in our galaxy.

We cannot grasp such numbers. But the matter is more complicated yet. Each neuron communicates with tens of thousands more. The numbers of connections is mind boggling. A neuron (see Figure 5) consists of three parts: a cell body with a nucleus, an axon and dendrites. The axon is a sort of communication cable surrounded by a myelin sheath to

Figure 6
The Junction between Neurons (Synapse)

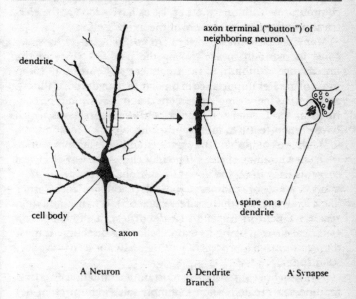

A Neuron   A Dendrite   A Synapse
                Branch

Adapted from D. Gareth Jones, Our Fragile Brains *(Leicester: Inter-Varsity Press, 1981), p. 40.*

insulate it because the cell sends electrochemical messages along the axon. Dendrites around the cell body, like sensors, bring electrochemical messages from other neurons, which are processed, integrated and sent on through the axon. At its far end the axon divides again to communicate with many more neurons, attaching itself to a spine of their dendrites or else to their cell bodies with fibers ending in little "buttons" or terminals (see Figure 6). These junctions between neurons are called synapses.

The Electrical Impulse

Before proceeding to describe in more detail how neurons communicate with one another, let us have a look at the electrical impulse that passes down the axon itself.

Many people with depressed friends or relatives have become increasingly aware during the past few years of the importance of lithium in the treatment of depression. Lithium is of greater importance in bipolar than in unipolar illness, and there is increasing agreement that its use should be confined to the former, or at least to those depressions which have certain features in common with bipolar illness.

While we still do not fully understand how lithium works, we have a number of clues. The first clue is the way electrical currents pass along the axons of neurons. Neurons are normally in a state of readiness to pass electrical messages (rather like a loaded gun with the safety catch off). When stimulation reaches a neuron (through its dendrites), it discharges an electrical current along its axon. Following discharge it must then go through a process of getting ready for its next volley, so to speak.

To grasp how this works we must understand that electrical readiness is created when common salt (sodium chloride) in the neuron is divided into its electrically charged components (sodium and chloride ions—or, as chemists would write it, $Na+$ and $Cl-$). When most of the sodium ions are on one side of the cell membrane and the chloride ions are on the other, a state of electrical tension exists along the membrane (similar to the electrical tension between storm clouds and the ground which gives rise to lightning). An electrical gradient has been created across it. The discharge of an electrical message along the length of the cell creates a domino effect as the sodium and chloride ions fall successively into one another's "arms" down the length of the axon (see Figure 7). Once this has happened a further current cannot be sent until the electrical gradient has been built up again along the whole

Figure 7
Passage of Current Along an Axon

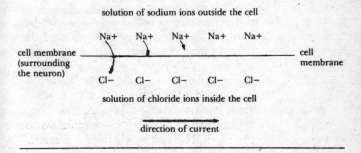

solution of sodium ions outside the cell

cell membrane (surrounding the neuron)

Na+   Na+   Na+   Na+   Na+

Cl–   Cl–   Cl–   Cl–   Cl–

cell membrane

solution of chloride ions inside the cell

direction of current

length of the cell membrane. Sodium ions and chloride ions have to "resume station" to be ready for the next electrical impulse.

In bipolar illness the mechanism begins to go wrong.[2] With depression the number of sodium ions increases by about 50% and with mania by about 150 to 200%. Too many ions are getting into the act. It seems likely that while transmission at the synapse (the space between one neuron and the receptor of another neuron) may be down, transmission along the axon is too sensitive. My diagram and the text may oversimplify matters. We still are not sure whether the number of available ions or their cellular distribution is the important factor. At any rate, lithium carbonate, an inert salt (whose use in mania was discovered by Cade in Australia) which takes no part in the passage of any electrical impulse, does seem to reduce the number of sodium and chloride ions to normal and thus to normalize neuronal transmission. Hence its great usefulness in bipolar illness.

Neurotransmitters–The Brain's Dispatch Riders
Now we can look more closely at the transmissions between

Figure 8
A Synapse

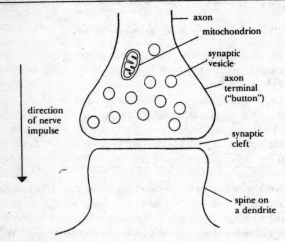

Adapted from D. Gareth Jones, Our Fragile Brains *(Leicester: Inter-Varsity Press, 1981), p. 43.*

neurons which occur at synapses (see Figure 6). A synapse basically consists of three parts: the terminal button of an axon, the dendrite of a neighboring neuron and a gap between the two (the synaptic cleft). (See Figure 8.) In the axon terminal are tiny "factories" called mitochondria which are involved in the production of neurotransmitters. When an impulse along an axon reaches the terminal, it triggers the release of neurotransmitters which are carried by synaptic vesicles to the synaptic cleft. Neurotransmitters are like dispatch riders, released from the axon terminal to speed across the intervening space and deliver their messages to the dendrite.

Why have I gone into so much detail? I have done so because depressive illness is associated with a depletion of neurotransmitters. The dispatch riders have mysteriously fallen in numbers. I say mysteriously because we do not fully know why this happens, any more than we know why they may spontaneously revert to normal after months or even years.

It is not that they are not *there*. They get "confined to barracks" in the terminals. Or the old ones are retired too quickly. Chemical tinkering corrects the matter by making access to barracks more difficult, thus keeping the dispatch riders on the job, or, alternatively, by insisting on later retirement for aging dispatch riders. The work of antidepressant medication (which I referred to as chemical tinkering) is of this sort. It keeps the supply of neurotransmitters at levels which permit normal brain function so that the depressed patients begin to recover their concentration, their energy, their sleep, their sex drive and all their other abilities, the lack of which has been crippling them.

Are there different breeds of neurotransmitters? In what specific areas do they operate? Are there specific barracks where they may be locked up or special keys to release them?

To such questions researchers are devoting more and more attention.[3] It seems likely that there are several types of neurotransmitter. Some scientists report a possible twenty neurotransmitters, others that the evidence may support as many as one hundred. Depressive illness may represent a relative shortage of one type but not necessarily of another. The most important ones seem to be norepinephrine, dopamine, serotonin and acetylcholine.[4] There is increasing evidence (though some disagreement about the evidence) that specific antidepressants release specific types of dispatch rider.

Release is really the wrong word, as is the word *barracks*. Scientists speak of storage spaces inside the buttonlike nerve endings. Tricyclic antidepressants (the commonest and the most powerful variety) seem to act not by releasing the neurotransmitters, but (as I described in the illustration of the dispatch riders) by slowing down the rate at which they can get back into their barracks. In this way more remain on the job or at least available to carry another message. Other anti-depressants (MAOIs) act by slowing the breakdown of neuro-transmitters (delaying the retirement of aging dispatch riders).

What effect all this has on the brain as a whole does not concern us except in the cases of memory and concentration, both of which can be seriously impaired in depressive illness. We are more concerned with the effects in and around the hypothalamus, a center deep in the brain mentioned earlier. The hypothalamus is important for two reasons. First, it contains the stop and go centers I have already mentioned, which have to do with appetite, sexual drive, sleep, weight gain and loss. Second, it is linked by blood canals to the pituitary gland (a tiny gland suspended from the hypothalamus and resting in a small bony cradle) which in turn regulates many body functions, many of them through the adrenal or suprarenal glands which sprawl comfortably around the top of the kidneys. When neurotransmitters are in short supply, vital body functions are impaired (see Figure 9). There is

Figure 9
How Neurotransmitters Affect Body Functions

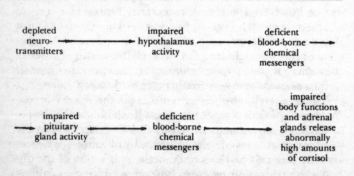

depleted neuro-transmitters → impaired hypothalamus activity → deficient blood-borne chemical messengers →

→ impaired pituitary gland activity ← deficient blood-borne chemical messengers → impaired body functions and adrenal glands release abnormally high amounts of cortisol even growing evidence that things like resistance to cancer may fall and that an increased susceptibility to cardiovascular disease may arise.

The link between hypothalamus, pituitary and adrenals has a simple application in depression.[5] Among the chemical agents, the adrenal glands themselves put out what is known as cortisol. The amount released increases in response to increased stress. An average person produces approximately the same quantity of cortisol every twenty-four hours. Most depressed persons put out much more.[6] Furthermore a depressed person's cortisol output reacts abnormally to administration of a cortisollike substance called dexamethasone. Dexamethasone suppresses a healthy person's cortisol levels. It does not suppress the raised cortisol levels of most depressed persons. Whether it does so depends on the chemical variety of illness from which the depressed person suffers. Thus our growing knowledge of the biochemistry of depression is slowly enabling us to distinguish different types of unipolar depression and to begin to treat them more rationally.

Genetics and Depressive Illness

To the biological models considered by Akiskal and McKinney we ought to add a genetics model, or at any rate to ask whether depressive illness can be inherited. Do depressive genes exist? Is future mental health determined at the moment of conception in the dark silence of the Fallopian tube?

Psychiatrists have been arguing about the question for about a century now, the "biological" psychiatrists presenting evidence upholding the importance of heredity and the psychologically minded psychiatrists challenging their position by evidence supporting the role of early environmental influences. Biological psychiatrists stressed *nature;* psychologically oriented psychiatrists, *nurture*.

The controversy is probably now out of date. In any case

we must be cautious in saying that any factor whether of nature or of nurture *determines* mental health. The most we can affirm is that one or the other may make some people susceptible to mental illness. We may say that some people have a greater risk of mental illness than others. A number of researchers express this by using the term *genetic loading* where inheritance is thought to be the source of the vulnerability.

As I review recent articles discussing the issue, it seems that there is a growing consensus that both nature and nurture (or heredity and environment, or again, genes and psychology) play a part, but that in some forms of depressive illness genetics may be more important while in other forms early experiences play the critical role.

In the previous chapter we looked at some of the evidence supporting the factors in early childhood that seemed to impart a predisposition to depressive illness. The volume of articles discussing the evidence for genetic factors as well as environmental factors is too voluminous for me to deal with it here. Perhaps one comment on the nature of modern studies will, however, be helpful. Not only are modern genetic studies more rigorous, but they show an increasing tendency to favor what are called *adoptive* studies, studies following up the psychiatric health of adopted infants whose natural parents suffered from depressive illness. The subsequent health of such children is compared with that of adopted children whose natural parents did not suffer from depressive illness. One excellent study of this kind was published by Remi Cadoret in 1978.[7]

Perhaps the most helpful way of considering the factors which expose us all to the risk of depressive illness is to consider the problem as I have represented it in Figure 10 on the next page. But it is time we turned from the nature/nurture question to a brief look at the morality of "tinkering with" the disordered brain chemistry we considered earlier in this chapter.

Figure 10
Influences Disposing People toward Depressive Illness

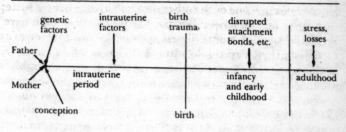

Ethical Questions

Have we any right to tinker with brain chemistry? Does doing so constitute mind control? Many of us have been alarmed by rumors of mind control in prisoners or students who have supposedly been subjected to experiments by scientists in prisons or other government agencies. The experiments have been justified in the name of science. Supposedly, the knowledge gained will benefit society as a whole.

The particular kind of tinkering we are talking about in this chapter is largely chemical. But morally there is no difference between psychological tinkering and chemical tinkering. Both have potential for abuse. Many people believe that psychiatry in Russia, for instance, is used to control both chemically and behaviorally political dissidents confined to mental hospitals.

Some years ago I heard an address by Uri Luryi, the renowned Soviet lawyer who defended several notable dissidents. The Luryis, having fled the Soviets, spent some time in Winnipeg while Luryi was on the faculty of law at the University of Manitoba.

From Luryi I learned not to judge Soviet psychiatrists. He made it clear that the psychiatrists with whom he dealt in his defense of dissidents were conscientious and not mere tools of the prosecution. He himself pointed out that all psychiatrists are influenced to some extent by the political environment they live in, whether in the East or the West, and expressed deep regret at the censure of Soviet psychiatrists by U.S. psychiatrists at a recent World Congress. His views are all the more remarkable when one reflects that Luryi is Jewish, that he defended Jewish dissidents, cross-examined non-Jewish Soviet psychiatrists, and finally that Luryi had to leave the Soviet Union and come to the West. Would such a man now safe in the West defend Soviet psychiatrists guilty of being political tools?

But the issue of psychiatry and brain control has also been raised in the United States. In October 1979 Federal District Judge Joseph Tauro issued a decision in Massachusetts affirming the patient's "right to refuse treatment," referring in his summary to "powerful and mind-altering drugs" and to what he termed "involuntary mind control." Clearly the questions raised are serious, and we must consider them carefully.

Two points should be borne constantly in mind. First, we are dealing with a delicate and marvelous instrument whose complexity defies our understanding. That is, it defies our *complete* understanding. Therefore, we must approach it with caution and respect. We have learned much. Brain function has become the focus of the most intense scientific endeavor in the world today. It attracts the brightest talent and is progressing in a way which would have been inconceivable twenty years ago. But our knowledge still leaves much to be desired. Second, the brain is more intimately connected with personality than other parts of our bodies. Certainly surgical intervention should be considered with extreme caution.

Yet have not those of us who are health professionals always been doing our best in spite of profound ignorance? Should we not, however cautiously, use those means God has placed at our disposal, and the knowledge he has given us, to help distressed and suffering people?

As a physician I must and I shall use what knowledge God has given me to alleviate the pain of depression. As chemical agents are placed in my hands that are able to restore the proper supply of brain neurotransmitters to depressed patients I will use them, bearing in mind always that what I do represents only one (but sometimes the most important and occasionally the only) means of healing depressed patients.

We must keep our perspective. We have only touched superficially on the astonishing marvels of brain and body as they relate to depression. But as human beings made in the image of God, we are not merely bodies. Treating depression is more than tinkering with brain chemistry. Depression affects the whole of us and the whole of us must be treated though sometimes our condition may call for one aspect of treatment more than another.

The legal problem arises in those cases where mental illness has reached the point of insanity. No Christian can approve of involuntary mind control of sane men and women. But many insane people inhabit a terrifying world of delusions. Definitions of psychosis differ. Usually psychosis (insanity) has to do with false perceptions of reality, such as to hear imaginary voices or to be gripped by delusional beliefs. And by delusional I mean beliefs that do not correspond to reality. Psychotic patients sometimes believe their friends and doctors (think of my little lady in chapter one) to be their tormentors and persecutors.

As psychiatrists we are confused about the borderline between what once was called neurosis and what still is called psychosis. To be psychotic implies impairment of one's understanding of reality, impairment which, as I have argued elsewhere, is associated with biochemical brain and body changes. Medications used to treat such changes are not mind-bending drugs but mind-straightening medications, restoring lucidity and clear thinking. As Appelbaum and Gutheil point out in their article, the U.S. Constitution can be interpreted to give patients the "right to rot."[8] Do we allow children the right to poison or burn themselves? Ought we to allow insane people to continue indefinitely in their worlds of terror? Would such interpretations have been the intention of lawmakers?

Before saying more about all the methods that exist for straightening bent minds, let us examine one of the darkest corners of depression—suicide.

8
The Anatomy
of Suicide

There is but one philosophic problem, and that is suicide. The task of man is to respond to life's apparent meaninglessness, despair, and its absurd quality.
Camus, "The Myth of Sisyphus"

He who is joined with all living has hope, for a living dog is better than a dead lion.
Ecclesiastes 9:4

Living is not good, but living well. The wise man, therefore lives as well as he should, not as long as he can. . . . He will always think of life in terms of quality, not quantity. . . . Dying early or late is of no consequence, dying well is. . . . Even if it is true that, while there is life there is hope, life is not to be bought at any cost.
Seneca

Before beginning this chapter I checked every Christian reference book in my library, including a systematic theology, Bible dictionaries and other likely theological treatises. Not one said a word about suicide. Perhaps this says more about the weakness of my library than anything else. Yet as I think about it I am convinced that the Christian taboo, the conspiracy of silence surrounding the topic of suicide is beyond any that used to keep sex under wraps. In three Christian bookstores I searched for books on suicide but found only David Wilkerson's book *Suicide*, stories of actual suicides among New York's disinherited.

"There are certain subjects about which we speak often in jest," Karl Menninger writes, "as if to forestall the necessity of ever discussing them seriously. Suicide is one of them. So great is the taboo on suicide that some people will not say the word, some newspapers will not print accounts of it, and even scientists have avoided it as a subject for research."[1] Among Christian writings I can remember an article on suicide in *Eternity* magazine some years ago. I know of an American IVP booklet (*Suicide* by Henri Blocher) and a moving article in the January 1980 issue of HIS magazine, but scratch my head as I might, I can think of nothing else. I have listened to hundreds, indeed thousands of sermons, but never one on suicide. All I can recall are occasional derogatory comments listing suicide among the evils of the society that surrounds us. Never from the pulpit have I heard any mention of Christians who commit suicide. Yet the first suicide I encountered was one committed by a warm-hearted follower of Christ, a medical student in my year, who was found dead in bed beside an empty bottle of sleeping pills.

After the funeral we all said wise things about how confused one gets after taking a sleeping pill. We commented reassuringly that it was so easy to take more and more, forgetting that one had already taken several. It was a tragic accident, we decided, collaborating with each other in an attempt to keep our deepest fears from surfacing. We could not bear the thought that our friend had told us repeatedly how dark his life had become, how far away God seemed, how hopeless everything was. We had listened and fed him earnest clichés. Was it our own failure we were concealing, or were we loyally trying to shield our friend and his family from disgrace?

One of my most treasured possessions is a copy of the Olney hymnbook, now out of print. It is a historical curiosity, begun by a poet, William Cowper, and John Newton. It was a venture Newton hoped would be "a monument to" their friendship. Each was to write a hymn every second week to be taught to

Newton's congregation in Olney, Buckinghamshire. Among Cowper's better known contributions are "There Is a Fountain Filled with Blood" and "Oh, for a Closer Walk with God."

But as I thumb through the book I find that the hymns written by Newton far outnumber those by Cowper. In the introduction to the edition in my collection Newton states, "We had not proceeded far upon our proposed plan, before my dear friend was prevented, by a long and affecting indisposition, from affording any further assistance."[2] Even in the hymn "Oh, for a Closer Walk with God" I notice the beginnings of his morbid disposition.

Where is the blessedness I knew
When first I saw the Lord?
Where is the soul-refreshing view
Of Jesus and His word?

The verse might pass for spiritual ardor if we did not know better. A later hymn reveals clearer signs of pathology.

The Lord will happiness divine
On contrite hearts bestow.
Then tell me, gracious God, is mine
A contrite heart or no?

I hear, but seem to hear in vain
Insensible as steel;
If aught is felt, 'tis only pain
To find I cannot feel.

Thy saints are comforted, I know,
And love thy house of prayer,
I therefore go where others go
And find no comfort there.

Cowper was often suicidal. Menninger cites an example from his pre-Christian days (from Winslow's *Anatomy of Suicide*, 1840).[3]

A friend procured him the situation of reading clerk to the House of Lords, forgetting that the nervous shyness which made a public exhibition of himself "mortal poison" would render it impossible for him ever to discharge the duties of his office. This instantly enveloped his faculties. At his request, his situation was changed to that of clerk of the journals; but even before he could be installed into office he was threatened with a public examination before the House. This made him completely wretched; he had not resolution to decline what he had not strength to do; the interest of his friend and his own reputation and want of support, pressed him forward to an attempt which he knew from the first could never succeed. In this miserable state, like Goldsmith's traveler "to stop too fearful, and too faint to go" he attended every day for six months at the office where he was to examine the journals in preparation for his trust. His feelings were like those of a man at the place of execution, every time he entered the office door; and he only gazed mechanically at the books, without drawing from them the least portion of information he wanted. As the time of his examination approached, his agony became more and more intense; he hoped and believed that madness would come to relieve him; he attempted also to make up his mind to suicide though his conscience bore stern testimony against it; he could not by any argument persuade himself that it was right; but his desperation prevailed, and he procured from an apothecary the means of self-destruction. On the day before his public appearance was to be made, he happened to notice a letter in the newspaper which to his disordered mind seemed like a malignant libel on himself. He immediately threw down the paper and rushed into the fields determined to die in a ditch; but the thought struck him that he might escape from the country. With the same violence he proceeded to make hasty preparations for his flight; but while he was engaged in packing his portmanteau his mind changed, and he threw himself into a coach, ordering the man to drive to the Tower wharf, intending to throw himself into the river, and not reflecting that it would be impossible to accomplish this purpose in that public spot, unobserved. On approaching the water, he found a porter seated upon some goods; he then returned to the coach and drove home to his lodgings in the Temple. On the way he attempted to drink the laudanum, but as often as he raised it, a convulsive agitation of his frame prevented its reaching his lips; and thus, regretting the loss of the opportunity, but unable to avail himself of it, he arrived half dead with anguish at his apartments. He then closed the door and threw himself on the bed with the laudanum near him, trying to lash himself up to the deed; but a voice within seemed constantly to forbid it; and as often as he extended his hand to the poison, his fingers were contracted and held back by spasms. At this time some of the inmates of the place came in, but he concealed his agitations; and as soon as he was left alone, a change came over him, and so detestable did the deed appear, that he threw away the laudanum and dashed the phial to pieces. The rest of the day was spent in heavy insensibility, and at night he slept as usual; but on waking at three in the morning, he took his penknife and laid with his weight upon it, the point being directed toward his heart. It was broken, and would not penetrate. At daybreak he rose, and passing a strong garter around his neck, fastened it to the frame of his bed. This gave way with his weight; but on securing it to the door he was more successful, and remained suspended until he had lost all consciousness of existence. After a time the garter broke, and he fell to the floor, so that his life was saved; but the conflict had been greater than his reason could endure. He felt a contempt for himself not to be expressed or imagined. Whenever he went into the street, it seemed as if every eye flashed upon him with indignation and scorn. He felt as if he had offended God so deeply that his guilt could never be forgiven, and his whole heart was filled with pants of tumultuous despair.

Cowper's suicide attempts were by no means over when he became a Christian. This gifted and godly man was used by the Holy Spirit to produce hymns that exalt the Lamb of God. Yet his own pitiful humiliation remains for us all to see. Let us be instructed by it, for Cowper is only one of many Christians who have struggled against the shame and horror of trying to take their own lives—some successfully, others unsuccessfully.

Scripture says remarkably little about suicide. It describes only four, and a possible fifth, all without comment. King Saul, defeated in battle and fearful of the mockery and torture of his enemies, fell on the point of his own sword. His armorbearer followed suit and died beside his master (1 Sam 31:4-6). Ahithophel, David's counselor who abandoned David only to have his counsel rejected by Absalom, went home, set his house in order, and hanged himself (2 Sam 17:23).

Judas Iscariot, after flinging the thirty pieces of silver back on the pavement before the chief priests and elders, also hanged himself (Mt 27:3-5). It is true that Jesus, speaking about Judas, said it would have been better for him never to have been born. But the words referred to his treachery to the Son of God. The suicide represented Judas's inability to come to grips with the appalling thing he had done. And who among us facing the horrible realization Judas faced might not have done as Judas did?

The fifth case is disputed as to whether it qualifies as a suicide. Samson died when he caused the collapse of the temple the Philistines were feasting in, killing three thousand men and women along with himself.

Suicide has been described as murder, murder of the self. For hundreds of years suicidal victims were refused burial in

Christian burial grounds. Laws arising in Christian countries generally treated attempted suicide as a crime, calling for trial and punishment on conviction. As recently as 1823 a citizen of London who committed suicide was buried at a crossroads in Chelsea with a stake pounded through his heart. In some cemeteries there is still a less sanctified section for suicides.

Yet the severity of Christians and the harshness of both civil and criminal law are surely reflections of human horror and dread rather than of obedience to God. Mercifully, the last thirty years have seen radical changes on the part of legal authorities and law-enforcement officers. In Britain the Suicide Act in 1961 decriminalized suicide (but increased penalties for any person aiding and abetting suicide). Even in places where suicide remains technically a crime, police and magistrates ignore the law and urge people who have attempted it to seek professional help.

Let us grant that suicide is not only tragic but sinful. Let us accept that life is a precious gift from God and that issues of life and death belong to their Author. But let us look on those who take their lives with the same compassion with which Jesus looked on all sinners. Indeed if compassion is called for, surely some suicide victims call for more compassion than other sinners.

Epidemiologists in the West have become increasingly convinced of the relationship between mental illness and suicide. Sainsbury[4] has argued from an impressive array of data that mentally ill people are special suicide risks. That is not to say that every person who commits suicide is mentally ill (though the phrase "disturbed balance of mind" must be true of most), but it is certain that many people in the West who commit suicide are. And with mental illness come impaired judgment, perceptual distortions and diminished volitional control. A recent review of 17 studies of patients who had suffered from depressive illness found that between 12 and 19% died by suicide.[5] Depressively ill people see reality through distorted spectacles. They are less able to make rational choices than the rest of us and should therefore be held less accountable for their actions. They are in great danger. When Barraclough and his colleagues reviewed one hundred consecutive suicides, they found that 93 of them were diagnosed as mentally ill and 80 were receiving treatment for mental illness.[6]

Every minute of every day, someone in the West succeeds in dying by his or her own hand. The number both of attempted and successful suicides increases year by year. It is a problem that Christians have largely ignored but one in which we should be eager to offer help.

Suicide and Society

Emil Durkheim, the brilliant French sociologist, produced the first sociological study on suicide. Arising from a careful examination of European vital statistics it remains influential to this day.[7]

Because Durkheim based his study on vital statistics, he has been justly criticized. Vital statistics are official records made in part from death certificates issued by doctors declaring the cause of death. Death certificates are notorious for underreporting suicide. Some authorities place the number of suicidal deaths at between ten and a hundred times as many as those reflected in vital statistics. Doctors and grieving relatives alike try to shield themselves from the tragedy of suicide. The underreporting of suicide undoubtedly varies from one society to another and from one country to another.

Nevertheless, Durkheim's incisive thinking, even though it was based on unreliable data, is impressive and influential. Two things strike me as I read his book. One is his very broad definition of suicide, and the other is his much quoted classification of types of suicide.

As a sociologist, Durkheim refused to be influenced by popular ideas about the morality of suicide or even its psychology. He interested himself only in those social patterns contributing to it. "The iconoclast, committing with the hope of a martyr's palm the crime of high treason known to be capital and dying by the executioner's hand, achieves his own death as truly as though he had dealt his own death blow. . . . Intent is too intimate a thing to be more than approximately interpreted by another. . . . It even escapes self-observation. How often we mistake the true reason for our acts."[8] So Durkheim included as suicide the deaths of soldiers defending their country and of mothers sacrificing their lives to save their children. "The term suicide is applied to all cases of death resulting directly or indirectly from a positive or negative act of the victim himself, which he knows will produce this result."[9] Most of us would prefer a narrower definition. But as a sociologist, Durkheim looked at every social circumstance which induced people to choose to die, stating, "At each moment of its history, therefore, each society has a definite aptitude for suicide."[10]

On examining nineteenth-century Swiss statistics he was fascinated by the difference between Roman Catholic and Protestant rates of suicide, which seemed to reflect religious rather than racial difference. (See Figure 11.)

Concluding that German-speaking Catholics committed more suicides than French-speaking Catholics not because of their blood "but because of the civilization in which they are reared," he hypothesized that the reason Protestants committed suicide more frequently lay in the emphasis on free in-

Figure 11
Suicide Rates per 100,000 Deaths

German-speaking Catholics 87	German-speaking Protestants 293
French-speaking Catholics 83	French-speaking Protestants 456

quiry and on the individual conscience among them. Roman Catholics, he thought, were more ready to accept their faith ready made. "All variation is abhorrent to Catholic thought. We thus reach our . . . conclusion, that the proclivity of Protestantism for suicide must relate to the spirit of free inquiry that animates this religion."[11] Two other factors he considered to be of importance were that Protestants were "a less strongly integrated church than the Catholic Church," and the fact that in nineteenth-century Europe education of the masses was more widespread among Protestants than among Catholics.

His reasoning may be based on unreliable data, but his conclusions are worth pondering. Consider his propositions:

1. Suicide varies inversely with the degree of integration of religious society.

2. Suicide varies inversely with the degree of integration of domestic society.

3. Suicide varies inversely with the degree of integration of political society.[12]

Do rising suicide rates reflect increasing social and family disruption? *Are Christians more prone to suicide when the churches they attend no longer constitute a closely knit supportive network?* The thesis sounds reasonable. Arguing that disintegration in any society throws individuals more on themselves, making them more inclined to guide their conduct by private criteria, Durkheim suggests that disintegration forces people to place greater priority on their own interests than on society's. He calls this egoism and suicides arising from it, egoistic suicides.[13] The term is not pejorative. As my links are severed from society's, I become a boat bobbing alone on life's seas. Under such circumstances it is inevitable that I pay more attention to my own little boat than to the flotilla of which I was once a part. And if storms arise I will be more intimidated by the waves, thinking even more of myself than of the flotilla from which I am separated and therefore succumbing to the waves in my isolation. "Egoism is not merely a contributing factor. . . . It is its generating cause. In this case the bond attaching man to life relaxes because that attaching him to society is itself slack."[14]

Durkheim adds two more types of suicide to egoistic suicide: altruistic suicide and anomic suicide. Altruistic suicide may seem at first to have little bearing on modern culture. It is suicide in the interests of society, sometimes at the coercion of society. In primitive tribes the aged who are no longer useful, and sometimes widows too, either starve themselves slowly or kill themselves. The followers of a great leader may take their lives when the leader dies.

How truly altruistic such suicides are is not always clear. Among the nomadic Ayoreos I visited in Bolivia, it was certainly true that the aged and sick would be a burden to the rest of the tribe in their jungle journeys. Yet the reason they gave for their suicides (for the old and the sick as well as for the twin babies who would be buried alive in shallow graves) was that it was dangerous to die above the ground. One needed a cover of earth for protection against evil spirits. So one missionary, horrified as for the first time he watched Indians shoveling earth onto a living, breathing old man, leaped into the grave to plead for the man's life. But his pleading was useless. The earth continued to fall and the old man made no attempt to escape, so that the missionary was obliged to climb out of the grave or be buried himself.

But altruistic suicide is a feature of complex as well as simple cultures. In India, Brahmins of bygone days were permitted to take their lives after a certain age and after fathering a son, and could be certain of a warm reception in the abode of Brahma. Jainists, as a religious rite, would starve themselves to death.

Altruistic suicide. Suicide for the benefit of society. We cite Oates's walking out into a blizzard during Scott's ill-fated Antarctic expedition so that the rest of the team could move faster and have more food. Do we also include Jonestown?

Anomic suicide may have more relevance for us. In his careful analysis Durkheim noted the relationship between economic crises and suicide, observing that suicides were associated not only with bankruptcy but also with suddenly acquired wealth.[15] Bankruptcy we can understand. But why do people who become suddenly rich take their lives?

Anomie (from Greek, meaning "without law") was described in terms of the disorientation and shock produced in people by an abrupt change in life, a change beyond anything they could have conceived, demanding new patterns of behavior in a new world where they had no chance to learn the rules. "Each in his sphere vaguely realizes the extreme limit set to his ambitions and aspires to nothing beyond. . . . Thus an end and goal are set to the passions."[16] We can be frightened, frightened to death in fact, when the world around us changes.

Many other sociologists have studied social patterns in relation to suicide since Durkheim's day, but some of his ideas persist. James Brown, a Canadian psychiatrist and suicidologist, noting the real increase in suicide attempts during recent years, suggested two possible reasons, Durkheim's anomie and the increase in alcoholism.[17]

It may be that the social disruption makes Camus's famous saying more relevant than Christians are willing to admit: "There is but one philosophic problem, and that is suicide. The task of man is to respond to life's apparent meaninglessness, despair, and its absurd quality."[18]

Technology is producing unnerving social changes, and the tempo of change increases constantly. Alvin Toffler (*Future Shock*) is not alone in drawing attention to it. Modern life disrupts communities and separates the wider family. Villages give place to cities. Local areas where small stores and a sense of community used to exist have been replaced by impersonal high-rise apartments, suburbs of isolated families and massive shopping centers. While some churches are dwindling, newer and progressive omnibus churches fail to give individuals a sense of belonging. Drive-in churches, electronic churches and the TV soap operas increasingly provide people with fantasy communities that are powerless to give warm support. A television set can never hug you. Modern Western technology increasingly provides the setting both for Durkheim's egoistic and his anomic suicides.

Suicide and Epidemiology

Whether differences in suicide rates reflect differences in the way doctors and relatives cover up suicide or whether the differences are real, statistics for the United States report an intermediate rate, exceeded by Austria, West Germany, Hungary, Japan, Czechoslovakia, Denmark, Finland, Sweden and Switzerland (some at more than twice the U.S. rate). On the other hand, Italy, the Netherlands and Spain all report lower rates than the United States.

Statistics also tell us that in many countries over the last two hundred years three times as many men have killed themselves as women. The same proportions apply for attempted suicide. Again, Black suicides in multiracial societies have always been fewer than White suicides.

During the seventies, however, new trends began to show. More women, more young people and more Black people committed suicide. Do the changes reflect the personal insecurities that arise from new roles that social changes have thrust on all three groups?

In 1972 Bagley published an interesting study which confirms Durkheim's idea of anomie. Using a measure of what he called authoritarianism, he rated 30 U.S. states and found that the degree of authoritarianism varied inversely with suicide rates.[19]

Brown had previously compared statistics in Canadian provinces and suggested that "there is a component in both accident rates and suicide rates that reflects a varying level of violent and unrestrained behavior in the communities." He notes that the outcome of these tendencies can be "delinquency, crime, drug dependence or suicide attempts."[20]

Brown is more hesitant in blaming alcohol. Yet a number of universally recognized statistics suggest that very correlation. In all areas of the Western world, about half the people brought to hospital emergency wards following a suicide attempt have been drinking. Suicides among alcoholics are far more common than among nonalcoholics. Alcoholism is rising in all Western countries, and alcohol disinhibits, that is, it removes fears and scruples.

For years I have been questioning people who attempt suicide after drinking. A minority tell me they planned the suicide and got drunk to make suicide easier and more pleasant. The majority are less clear. A more common story is, "I've been feeling down for a long time. I just took a few drinks. I wasn't really planning to take the pills...." More solid evidence comes from California where the rate has increased and decreased in exact proportion to the annual consumption of alcohol.[21]

Who commits suicide? Who is likely to be successful and who to fail? Twenty years ago most psychiatrists would have told you that men are more successful in their suicide bids (they tended to use guns and hanging more frequently) than women, and that the aged were more successful than the young.

Among people diagnosed as depressed, the successful suicide rate has been calculated at 551 per 100,000 for patients over 55 and 159 per 100,000 for patients under 55.[22] Widows and widowers, often sick and alone, were common victims. But, as I mentioned above, patterns are changing. Women are beginning to catch up with men and young people with the aged.

The latest suicide trends are frightening. Until recently it seemed that suicide risk increased progressively with age.

But since the 1950s increasing numbers of adolescents and people in their early twenties have been killing themselves. Adolescent suicides are now commoner in many areas than suicides of the aged.

A question arises. Is suicide risk now peaking at an earlier age? Or may we expect that today's adolescents as a group will become more and more suicidal as they grow older? If the answer to the second question is yes, the number of suicides will increase horrendously over the next forty years. This is precisely what statisticians predict. Examining the progress of five-year cohorts (people whose births fall within five years of one another) as they age, two studies—one of Alberta and another of the whole of the United States—indicate that since 1951 the suicide rate in these younger age groups has increased progressively over time.[23] Suicide is already the second commonest cause of death among youth in some areas. The prospect of an advancing wave of suicides fills us with dismay.

Doctors are frequently reported to have the highest suicide rate among professionals and pastors the lowest. Walter Freeman, who once reviewed the obituary columns of the *Journal of the American Medical Association* between 1895 to the recent past begins his report with bald statements: "Doctors of medicine are more prone to suicide than are men in other occupations. Psychiatrists appear at the top of the list." But the statistics on doctors' suicides have been challenged.[24] Doctors, of course, have expert knowledge on how to be successful and have the means of suicide constantly at their disposal.

Among doctors, pediatricians are said to have the lowest suicide rate and psychiatrists the highest.[25] Blachly agrees with Freeman who comments, "The high rate in psychiatrists is undoubtedly influenced by preselection. The psychiatrist being in frequent intense emotional relationships with patients (including suicidal patients) learns better than most that suicide is a way of solving problems."[26] Freeman went on to explain why suicides, especially among psychiatrists over sixty, are almost certainly higher than the obituary columns of the *JAMA* report stating, "In older psychiatrists, suicide is a logical termination of life at the time when hope has been abandoned."[27]

But do not other older men also lose hope? To this day the number continues to increase as men grow older. In Canada for instance, the suicide rate for men over sixty-five is between 30 and 40 per 1,000 of the population. For men under fifty it is between 12 and 13.[28] Why then should psychiatrists be peculiarly prone to suicide as they grow older? An editorial in the *British Medical Journal* is of the opinion that among people who choose psychiatry as a career are some who have a morbid curiosity into the murky depths of their own psyches and may therefore be increasingly appalled by what they find: "Some who take up psychiatry probably do so for morbid reasons."[29]

Happily, the rate among psychiatrists in training is no different from those of other physicians in training, which in turn does not differ from other people of similar age in the general population.[30] Despite this fact, the suicide tendencies among practicing psychiatrists raises an important question. The practice of counseling is increasing and has now become a profession. Are we going to see rising suicide rates among educational and pastoral counselors? Or is there something unique to psychiatric counseling which exposes psychiatrists to the danger of suicide?

Psychology of Suicide

So far we have looked at the sociology and, to a limited extent, the epidemiology of suicide. It is perhaps time we turned to the narrower concerns of psychologists and psychiatrists in their attempts to understand what motives, conscious or unconscious, drive men and women into the arms of death. Let us first look at conscious motives. What reasons do survivors from suicide give for their actions?

This afternoon a young man of twenty told me, "I wanted to make them all sorry for me."

"Wanted to make whom sorry, your family?"

"No, my friends. They wouldn't help me find a girlfriend. So I felt the only thing to do was to kill myself. Then they'd be sorry."

I suppose we could say his motive was one of revenge, revenge on friends who had failed to give him what he wanted. Many patients give me similar reasons.

Often after they recover consciousness I ask them, "How do you feel about still being alive? Do you want to live?" Some tell me they don't know. I ask them, "What would it be like to be dead?" and the most pathetic, yet the most chilling and dangerous answer is, "Peace. I'll be at peace when I die." Others reply, "Just nothing. Nothing at all." Such people are those most likely to try again, unless they can be helped to see things differently.

Others have told me, "I deserve to die. I'm not worthy to live." To them death constitutes some kind of atonement for what they see as their failures and sins. Most patients who tell me this are profoundly depressed.

Many who seem merely to be playing with the idea of death (that is, those who give evidence of not really wanting to die but are like the man I talked with this afternoon) want to impress others and are seeking some kind of change. Men threaten to shoot themselves when their wives leave them and, having made sure someone will find them, sit holding a loaded gun to their heads. Similarly, wives whose husbands are unfaithful turn up in the emergency room having taken an overdose of pills.

Two things become apparent as their stories are carefully evaluated. One is that the attempt was manipulative, designed to affect their spouse's behavior. The other is that the device often succeeds, at least for the time being. Erring husbands make earnest promises to change. Errant wives anxiously return.

The game, however, is dangerous. One may miscalculate with disastrous consequences—taking too big a dose or having the trigger of a gun squeezed in the struggle to withdraw it. Manipulative suicide attempts are like crying wolf. After the third or fourth suicide attempt, spouses become hardened and resentful, growing angrier with each succeeding visit to the hospital.

One must never assume that the number of pills taken represents the seriousness of the attempt. "I took five Dalmane," one woman told me. There was something deathly tranquil about her.

"Why five?" I asked.

"Because I knew that was enough to kill me."

She clearly meant what she said. I took care *not* to tell her that she could have taken many more and come to no harm. I'd rather she stick to Dalmane if she has any more suicidal urges.

One boy spent hours alone, sitting with a loaded shotgun, the open end of the barrel in his mouth while he played with the trigger.

"What made you do it?"

"I dunno. Maybe there is a heaven. Maybe it'll be better there. Who knows?"

"What were you thinking of when you sat with a gun in your mouth?"

"I was trying to get up my courage. I'd think I'd do it, then I'd get scared and think about it some more. Is there a better life after death? I guess nobody knows, eh? Anyway it couldn't be worse than this life."

That young man survived several serious attempts on his life. Perhaps he is a compulsive gambler, excited by the big stakes in the suicidal game. Unfortunately, his compulsion shows no tendency to decrease.

Some of my patients tell me, "The voices were telling me to do it. They said, 'Get a rope and hang yourself!' They just kept saying it."

One girl, agitated and weeping, said, "I have to be crucified, like Jesus, and then there won't be any war."

"What makes you think that?"

"The voices—I'm sure they were angels—told me. I don't actually have to get on the cross. Just so long as I die. Maybe I *am* Jesus. . . ."

Many leave notes (usually an indication of the seriousness of the attempt) in which phrases like, "You'll be much better off without me," "It will be all for the best," "This is the way it has to be" and "I love you," frequently occur. The handwriting is often unsteady, suggesting the writer was intoxicated either from alcohol or sedatives or both, sinking toward unconsciousness even while they wrote. Sometimes the note is unfinished, ink trailing in an unsteady line as death supervened.

Some people are confused about their reasons for suicide. They felt desperate. Didn't know what to do. Were "mixed up." As I sit and listen I begin to discover they wanted help with their problems but didn't know how to ask for help, or else had no one to turn to. The phrase "a cry for help" has been used to describe them.

A British study followed 189 depressed, young, mostly White females for ten months. They noticed the young women were hostile, had previous suicide attempts, and abused drugs and alcohol. During the ten months twelve of them made suicide attempts, one of which was successful.[31] Other workers have implicated hostility in suicide bids. Weismann and colleagues compared 29 suicidally depressed women with 29 nonsuicidally depressed women and found the suicidal group were significantly more hostile. They also found excessive drug use in the suicidal group.[32] Yet one wonders whether both groups (younger, predominantly White women) were characteristic of depressed or suicidal patients as a whole. Perhaps they form what one might call a subgroup among the suicidal population.

In *Man against Himself*, Karl Menninger, writing lucidly and interestingly, harks back to the retroflexed-rage views of Abraham and Freud. While freely admitting the complexity of the subject, he reduces suicide to three basic drives.

1. The wish to kill.
2. The wish to be killed.
3. The wish to die.

First, Menninger reminds us that murder lurks deep within the shadows of every human heart, murder that the murderer might survive. He sees (a thought which will shock mothers) nursing as a cannibal act, as the baby consumes part of the mother. Second, he sees the wish to be killed as an extreme form of submission, arising from unconscious guilt and the need to be punished. Third, he also reminds us that it is easier to vent our murderous rage on ourselves than on someone else. (He may have a point. One of my patients, when depressively ill, beats himself with his own fists.) The wish to die is sometimes not strong enough, and its lack of strength accounts for the many failed suicides.

He also points to the ambivalence which most psychiatrists and psychologists agree is common to many people attempting suicide by quoting an amusing but macabre article from *Time* (November 17, 1930). Mr. Q. R. S. of Los Angeles first tried "to hang himself from a chandelier. The chandelier came down. He cut his throat and still lived. He slashed his wrists and still lived. He opened the veins at his elbows. When two detectives and a doctor came he was pronounced dead. Then Q. R. S. jumped out of bed, began fighting all three."[33]

Menninger, in viewing suicide along with Freud as inwardly turned aggression, is automatically giving the same explanation to suicide as he does to depressive illness. Unquestionably, depression and suicide are linked, but depressed people are tortured by a bewildering set of feelings and impulses. Perhaps we shall never be able to point to simple causes of suicides, but it is instructive to look at the many ideas and impulses in the minds of those who commit it.

Clues to their thoughts are given by those who leave notes. Others who make desperate bids (like throwing themselves under a train) sometimes survive. Insofar as they understand their own motives, they describe them. Occasionally, in the dreams that haunt them in the nights leading up to their attempts, we find insight. Among the many reasons for suicide and suicide attempts in psychological literature are the following:

1. An attempt to atone for wrongdoing.
2. Escape from an intolerable situation.
3. A vindictive wish to hurt others.
4. Masochism—torture ending in death, inflicted for the sexual ecstasy experienced at the point of death.
5. The wish to find peace or a better life.
6. Desire to rejoin a loved one.
7. An attempt to communicate to others the suicide's feeling of desperation ("a cry for help").
8. A last-ditch attempt to manipulate or control a situation. (It is surprising how far some people will go to impose their will on others.)
9. The "fun" of gambling.

In all suicides, some degree of ambivalence exists, the wish to die competing with the desire to live; consequently, it becomes difficult to define a suicide attempt. Some people who take an overdose of pills or who scratch their wrists with razors seem to have little wish to die and say so following their attempt. Yet the thought of death was in their minds. They were playing with death, and in so doing demonstrating some degree of contempt for life.

Sometimes the term *suicidal gesture* is used, often in muttered contempt toward younger people who have been drinking before their "gestures" and who clutter busy emergency wards where harried nursing and medical staffs are trying to cope with accident victims and people requiring emergency care for heart attacks. Who has time under such conditions for a "suicidal gesture"?

The more serious the attempt, the more likely it is that the sufferer is mentally ill, either seriously depressed or schizophrenic (deluded, in despair or obeying hallucinatory voices). Since the early 1960s Beck, whom I mentioned in chapter six, has been focusing on hopelessness as the one special feature in the depressed mood which could be a key to an understanding of suicide and even a help in preventing it. Hopelessness is not the feeling of depression on which we should focus; the distorted view of reality is. Hopelessness is a cognitive process. It is seeing things wrongly. The suicidal person suffers from a mistaken thought.

Minkoff, one of his coworkers, has produced, in addition to Beck's Depression Inventory, a hope scale called a General Expectancies Scale. In a small trial they have demonstrated a relationship between the General Expectancies Scale and another scale, the Suicidal Intent Scale (designed to assess the degree or seriousness of suicide intent). To Minkoff, Beck and their coworkers, hope and suicide intent can be measured scientifically, and according to their studies, the less hope there is, the greater the risk of suicide.[34]

Yet how useful is this information? How easy is it to teach a suicidal person to "think straight" about the future? To what extent is crooked thinking a result of a disturbed mood? Can disturbed thinking (as Beck claims) be corrected and mood changed? Often I find that disturbed thinking is the result, not the cause, of disturbed emotions.

Suicide: Fact and Fable
If suicides are to be reduced in number, the problem must be tackled on many levels. Where possible, closely knit and

structured communities must be developed. If political and general social changes cannot effect this, then local churches can at least examine themselves to see how they can become the communities they are meant to be.

Mental illness must be treated early and more vigorously. Psychiatrists, doctors and counselors of all kinds must be better trained in handling such illnesses and be made more aware of the dangers of suicide.

In 1974 Barraclough decided to take a look at all that had happened in the lives of 100 recent suicides. The list below gives some of his findings:

93 had visited a doctor within one year of death.
69 had visited a doctor within one month of death.
48 had visited a doctor within one week of death.

75 had visited their family doctor within one year of death.
59 had visited their family doctor within one month of death.
40 had visited their family doctor within one week of death.

24 had visited a psychiatrist within one year of death.
18 had visited a psychiatrist within one month of death.
11 had visited a psychiatrist within one week of death.

55 had talked recently about death, dying or suicide.

34 had made suicide threats during the previous year.
21 had made suicide threats within the previous month.
13 had made suicide threats within the previous week.

The list should not make us critical of the doctors and relatives concerned, but they should make all of us more alert to the realities of suicide. Psychiatrists and emergency officers, as we shall see later, are often in a no-win situation when dealing with those threatening suicide. But we must all realize that suicide talk usually preceeds suicide actions.

Schneidman contrasts a series of what he calls fables and facts in his section on suicide in the *Comprehensive Textbook of Psychiatry*.[35]

Fable: People who talk about suicide do not commit suicide.

Fact: Of every 10 persons who kill themselves, 8 have given definite warning of their intentions.

Fable: Suicide happens without warning.

Fact: Studies reveal that the suicidal person gives many clues and warnings regarding his suicidal intentions.

Fable: Suicidal people are fully intent on dying.

Fact: Most suicidal people are undecided about living or dying, and they gamble with death, leaving it to others to save them. Almost no one commits suicide without letting others know how he is feeling.

Fable: Once a person is suicidal, he is suicidal forever.

Fact: Persons who wish to kill themselves are suicidal only for a limited period of time.

Fable: Improvement after a suicidal crisis means that the suicidal risk is over.

Fact: Most suicides occur about 3 months after the beginning of improvement, when the person has the energy to put his thoughts and feelings into effect.

Fable: Suicide strikes much more among the rich, or conversely almost exclusively among the poor.

Fact: Suicide is represented proportionately among all levels of society.

Fable: Suicide is inherited or runs in the family.
Fact: It is an individual pattern.

Fable: All suicidal patients are mentally ill.
Fact: Studies of hundreds of suicide notes indicate that, although the suicidal person is extremely unhappy and always perturbed, he is not necessarily ill.

Some of Schneidman's facts call for qualification. Although most suicidal people are ambivalent toward death, we must be wary of the idea that it is always possible to stop someone from committing suicide. It is not. I have known a cleverness and a determination in some suicidal persons that has outwitted the most experienced professionals.

I think of one woman who had made so many repeated and determined efforts to kill herself that she was accompanied by special nurses twenty-four hours a day. She liked to use bath cubes in her tub and to see plenty of foam beneath which she could luxuriate. One day as she was apparently enjoying her usual relaxation in the tub, she used the long and sharpened fingernail of her right forefinger to pierce the skin of her left wrist, severing her radial artery. The warmth of the bathwater encouraged a rapid flow of blood from the severed artery while white foam concealed the reddened water. By the time her nurse (secure in the knowledge that it was "impossible" for her to harm herself while she was watching) became suspicious of her drowsiness and strange pallor, it was too late to save her. I have known of other equally ingenious and determined attempts where suicide took place in spite of the utmost vigilance.

Her death raises a question. Had she not a right to choose death? Were we violating her human rights? I believe not. God created her. He alone possessed the right to dispose of her life. Her body belonged to him.

While Schneidman is also correct that a suicidal person is not necessarily mentally ill, many suicidal patients are. At the depth of their depression some patients, dragged down by the psychomotor retardation I referred to earlier, are unable to muster enough energy even to take their lives. Yet within two to five weeks, as improvement begins and energy increases, a sudden (almost joyful) calm alerts the sensitive observer to danger. The calm may be the calm of a resolution firmly taken—to commit suicide.

Thus it is true that after some improvement has begun (I presume Schneidman's expression "about 3 months" represents some sort of average), danger still exists. My own experience indicates there is another danger besides that of early improvement. It exists among patients whose depression is inadequately treated. Such a patient may be released from the hospital, perhaps on inadequate doses of medication and inadequately supervised by their therapists. Though improved, such patients are prey to bouts of despair as they struggle to face life's demands with inadequate resources. Most who kill themselves do so during the first six months following their release from the hospital. But a significant number do so during the first two years.

Menninger may be referring to such patients when he states, "Patients committed to our care in the depth of a temporary depression in which they threatened suicide would begin to improve, and relatives thereupon would seek to remove them, utterly disregarding our warning that it is too soon, that suicide was still a danger. Frequently they would ridicule the idea that such a thing might be perpetrated by *their* relative.... Then a few days or weeks later, the paper would carry an announcement of our former patient's death by hanging or shooting or drowning."[36]

Finally, Schneidman's contention that suicide does not "run in the family" is a half-truth. True, every suicide stands alone. It is the act of one person. Nevertheless, I have certainly found a pattern of suicide in some families. Recently, for instance, I spent time with a middle-aged Native American couple bowed down with the grief of family suicides. Both were evangelical Christians and active Christian workers living and working on a reservation. Their son was in the hospital following a bid to hang himself from a tree near the reservation, a tree known locally as the "hanging tree." One year previously his uncle had hung himself from its branches. Eleven months later (just a month before my patient's attempt), his cousin's corpse had been found dangling from the same branch of the same tree. My patient must surely have been influenced by these events. Needless to say, members of the tribe cut the tree down.

Suicide can have a powerful and devastating effect upon anyone close to the person who commits it. If the vulnerability to depression runs in the family, it is almost inevitable that any family members who fall prey to the illness will begin to let their thoughts drift toward suicide. They may resist the thoughts. They may firmly resolve never to follow the example of their ill-fated relative. Fear and fascination, however, will draw their thoughts to what happened in the past and what could happen again.

Before leaving Schneidman's fables and facts, let me add one of my own.

Fable: Deep religious faith makes suicide impossible.

Fact: The despair and hopelessness accompanying severe depressive illness can undermine faith. Godly patients have looked me in the eye and told me despairingly, "My faith has gone." Such is the vulnerability of our bodies and brains to minute chemical changes, and so delicate is the balance between madness and sanity that the strongest Christians can become victims of suicidal despair.

At such a time it is not faith they need, but the ministrations of the skillful and the faithful, to watch over them until the proper balance of their minds is restored and with it the faith they thought they had lost.

There are a number of possible ways by which we may try to reduce the number of suicides. This is the topic of the next chapter.

Part IV
Coping with
Depression & Suicide

9
Coping with Suicide

Then [Job's] wife said to him, "Do you still hold fast to your integrity? Curse God, and die." But he said to her, "You speak as one of the foolish women would speak. Shall we receive good at the hand of God, and shall we not receive evil?"... And Job died, an old man, and full of days.
Job 2:9-10; 42:17

It is one thing to understand depressive states, even to perceive the need of a depressed person. It is quite another to help them. And nowhere is help more critical than when depressed friends or colleagues have thoughts of taking their lives.

How should suicidal people be handled? Perhaps the first step is to try to assess how great the risk is. Let me review some of the factors I mentioned in the last chapter as we consider ways to assess the danger of suicide.

Assessing Suicidal People
Age. In spite of recent trends, it remains true that the older

the person the greater the risk of successful suicide.

Sex. Men still succeed more often in killing themselves than women.

Isolation. The lonelier the suicidal person, the greater the risk of suicide. Adults with children or people surrounded by family and friends are less likely to take their own lives.

Physical and mental health. People suffering from serious debilitating illness, or who suffer from major depression or schizophrenia are more at risk.

Family history. Those whose friends and close relatives have committed suicide are also more at risk.

Drugs and alcohol. Alcohol in particular disinhibits. Intoxicated people do things they would not dare do when sober— including trying to take their lives.

Availability. The more easily suicidal people can get at the means of killing themselves, the greater is the risk that they will use them.

A suicidal man or woman is not a statistic but a human being. Persons assessed as "seriously suicidal" may never take their lives and persons judged "mildly suicidal" may. Averages do not apply to individuals, nor can human actions be predicted with certainty.

Casualty officers in the emergency departments of general hospitals face the dilemma of having to assess far more suicidal patients than there are hospital beds to accommodate them. Inevitably many patients who have attempted suicide or who come for help because of their suicidal thoughts have to be turned away from the hospital. Psychiatrists and casualty officers live in dread of the day when a local newspaper headline will read, "Man Turned Away from Hospital Shoots Himself," for it is impossible to admit all persons who have tried to kill themselves, to say nothing of those who only say they might. So however difficult it may be to predict suicide accurately, some rough attempt must be made to assess in whom the risk is gravest. Thus an elderly widower, who has for months been eating and sleeping poorly, who recently has been drinking more, who lives alone and is childless, who was told a few weeks ago that he had cancer and who keeps a loaded gun by his bed should be taken more seriously than a thirty-year-old woman brought to an emergency room after an overdose of Valium who is crying hysterically because her husband has left her and her children for the third time.

The most reliable indicator of suicide is what people say and how they say it. When someone tells you in a low voice that there is no hope, no other way or that they long for peace, you must take them very seriously. When they make a great to-do about their intentions using suicide as a threat to get their own way, they should still be taken seriously, but less so.

Dealing with Suicidal People

I may have made a serious mistake this afternoon. I was talking to a thirty-five-year-old secretary, single parent of two boys—one a troublesome fourteen-year-old, the other nine. Monica (not her real name) had avoided me for three months, began the interview guardedly and then let me know that she was sleeping three hours a night and thinking what it would be like to die as she tossed and turned, waiting for dawn to break.

I had quite a job finding what lay behind the quiet facade she presented. She was frightened of being hospitalized and worried about my reaction to what she would say. An earnest Christian, she eventually said, "I've been giving a lot of thought to—uh—ending it all, . . ." then with a big breath, " . . . and I don't really see that it's as wicked as they make out."

"How were you thinking of doing it?"

My mind wandered. Monica didn't play games, except in the sense of never leveling completely with me, calculating in her mind how much she could tell me and still not be forced into the hospital. This time she evaded my question. "I'm really trying, you know. I'm not as bad as I was a week ago."

Monica meant that she was trying to fight her depression and that she was beginning to succeed.

The interview went on. I felt we were sparring guardedly. I made at least five more attempts to penetrate her defenses, but she wouldn't give.

"I would want it to be peaceful," she said eventually.

"Pills?"

She said nothing.

"What do you have available?"

"Dalmane."

I breathed a little more easily. "How many?"

"About a hundred."

She cried quietly as we talked about electroconvulsive therapy (ECT). I had made many previous trials of antidepressants with her, all without success. ECT on the other hand had produced dramatic changes. Frustrated, she said, "I come here trusting you, and you, you drive me into a corner."

"You feel I am punishing you?"

"Yes. I've always felt that way about ECT. And I'm trying so hard!"

My attempts to reassure her were in vain. The stigma of hospitalization on a psychiatric ward and her fear of ECT, which she had twice, made her shrink into herself.

"I'm going to hospitalize you."

She rallied her remaining resources. Weariness and fear showed in her face. "No, Dr. White, please don't do that. Please, *please* don't do that. I couldn't stand it. If ever that happened to me. . . . I'll come back to see you in a week. I promise I won't do anything."

I was troubled. My conscience was telling me I shouldn't give in to her. Yet I felt myself weakening. "What would death be like?" I asked her eventually.

"I get so tired. There seems no end to it."

There was a long pause. "Peace?" I asked.

She nodded slowly. "Yes, that's it. Peace."

We prayed together. I can remember nothing of her prayer. I think I was probably arguing with myself about my responsibility while Monica prayed. In any case I have difficulty hearing her when she prays, so low does her voice sink.

After she left I was still ambivalent. I know her well, and what I hope is a reliable hunch told me she would not do anything before her next visit. But I could not be sure. I nervously figured the odds for survival on taking a hundred Dalmane. I called her pastor (we have a working arrangement of which Monica is aware) and alerted a colleague who knows her almost as well as I do. But I will not sleep soundly for the next six nights.

Yet even in the hospital it is difficult to manage very suicidal patients. I have already discussed the difficulties of preventing a really determined person from committing suicide. In some hospitals they have a policy of removing belts, ties, shoelaces, razor blades, nailfiles—anything and everything that could be used to strangle, cut or in any way harm the suicidal patient. Such precautions, however, can be humiliating and dehumanizing to someone whose self-esteem is already low. Walking around a locked ward with no laces in your shoes and holding your pants up (if you're a man) can give you an abysmal sense of wretchedness. It is kinder to preserve the dignity of a suicidal person, but how safe is it? Doctors may leave orders on a chart requiring "suicidal observation" on such patients, but who wants an anxious nurse hanging around the toilet every time you go there? What do you say when someone asks, "Are you O.K.?" every five minutes. And it can take less than five minutes to kill yourself.

Tact, understanding, frankness and courtesy can mean much to suicidal people. It is better to be frank about the issues involved and show some degree of trust. There is no cast-iron method of preventing someone's suicide. Excessive zeal and fear on the part of the helping persons are self-defeating and should be tempered with understanding of the patient's needs. Our fears and our officiousness serve to isolate patients already wrapped in aloneness. We divide ourselves into two groups, those of us who fear and those whose suicidal urges fill us with fear. Our fear must be tempered with warmth and understanding.

The treatment of suicidal persons will depend on the nature and severity of their difficulties. If they are ill, their sickness must be diagnosed accurately and treated promptly. If the risk is grave in a patient with depressive illness, the fastest, safest and quickest method is ECT. Its advantages and disadvantages will be discussed in the next chapter. When such patients recover fully, it is hard for them to believe that the nightmare temptation could have been so alluring. In fact, they prefer to push the matter to the back of their minds.

I have made it clear that one of the best ways to prevent suicide is to treat promptly and vigorously any underlying depressive illness. In the same way, the prevention of future suicides will include encouragement to seek help early, as soon as depression begins, and in some cases to make regular visits to a competent professional.

Disturbed people are not always willing to seek professional help. Civil libertarians all over the West are busy seeking amendments to law in the direction of what are called "patient rights," and of giving all citizens the right to freedom from help they neither seek nor want. Some as I mentioned before, would even argue for the individual's right to commit suicide.

Certainly "mental" patients have at times been subject to gross abuse. While the movie *One Flew Over the Cuckoo's Nest* reflects conditions of thirty years ago rather than of the present, it is salutary that we be warned. Nevertheless, there is a gap between liberty from unwarranted coercion and irresponsible abandonment of desperate and needy people. Thousands of people who a few weeks ago sought to kill themselves are today profoundly glad they were rescued from death. I see the gratitude in the faces of such people every day, and I am grateful that law permits me forcefully to restrain such people from suicide. I urge you to do all you can strongly to encourage any friend or relative who is depressed and has hinted at suicide to get competent help from a qualified counselor, social worker, psychologist or psychiatrist. If your attempts are unsuccessful and if state or provincial laws allow for enforced treatment, then do not hesitate to request the use of force.

Many persons, though, who attempt suicide are not suffering from a depressive illness. How can they be helped? The question is important, for studies as well as clinical experience teach us that many people after their first attempt may make repeated suicide bids. If you talk to such people, you will find that there seems to be a curious emotional detachment from their brush with death. They may be grateful to be alive, alert and happy, but curiously hazy about their feelings prior to the suicide bid. You would suppose that their near miss could form the basis for increased self-understanding and a consequent prevention of future suicidal urges. More commonly, people have carefully sealed off the horrifying memories of their feelings and behavior.

One method of treating patients who have attempted suicide was described by Reznik and his colleagues[1] who videotaped patients admitted to the hospital for suicide attempts, recording their words, their facial expressions, their initial reactions to attempts to save them. When patients were shown the videotapes later, they were angry, attempting futilely to deny the reality they witnessed. They would turn their rage on the therapist, but later, as their anger cooled, they would begin to accept what had happened and to gain more insight into their problems. Whether the method will be effective in preventing future suicide attempts remains to be seen.

Return for a moment to the problem of what to do when,

as a counselor (trained or untrained), you are faced with someone who may be suicidal and who may use the threat of suicide as moral blackmail. How can you be sure of the true state of affairs? Perhaps the first rule is: If you are uncertain, check with someone with more experience, and do not ever allow yourself to be manipulated into "not telling anybody."

No two people contemplating suicide are alike. Yet it is possible to divide people thinking of suicide into a couple of broad groups. There are those who are quick to talk suicide and who use it as a threat or as a manipulative device to get their own way, to regain the affections of an angry lover or to awaken sympathy. The danger in dealing with such people is that they may awaken feelings of hostility in us so that in an angry moment we may say, "Well, go ahead and do it then!" driving them to fulfill their own threat, if only to prove to us that they meant it.

Others are more reluctant to talk. The rule in their case is to force yourself to overcome your embarrassment about a distasteful subject and *ask*. In the delicate case where your friend has not even hinted at suicide, except in the sense that he or she is telling you how deeply disheartened he or she is, so that your suspicions are aroused of a true depression, the danger is more serious. Squelch your hesitancy. Ask. Say to your friend, "Have you ever thought of harming yourself?" or "Has the thought of suicide ever crossed your mind?" The response will be immediate. Either it will be "Oh, *no*. No, no. Nothing like that. I just wouldn't!" Or, perhaps in a relieved whisper, relieved because he or she wanted you to bring it up, the answer will be "Yes. Yes, I guess I have." Your friend, believe it or not, will almost always be glad to share what to him or her is an intolerable burden, the burden of deciding "to be or not to be."

Then you must ask, "Have you just thought about it, or have you gone as far as planning it? How serious are your thoughts?" Don't hint. Don't beat around the bush. This is the time for direct questions, and in nine cases out of ten you will get direct answers. The more direct the answer, the more seriously you must take it.

If the answer should be, "Well, not exactly planned, but I do think a lot about it," you must ask, "How have you thought of doing it?" If your friend says, "Pills," your next questions must be "Do you have any?" and "What kind are they and how many do you have?" Remember, the same pills that can alleviate a depression can also kill. The doctor who prescribes them should always calculate the suicidal risk before deciding how many to prescribe.

If it is a gun you must ask, "Where is your gun? Do you have ammunition for it?" Hanging or drowning are more elusive, but you must press on with questions. Why? Only thus will you know how far the details have been thought out and whether the means are available. Is there a rope? Where would your friend hang? Is there a river? A bridge? An accessible window to jump from?

With the manipulative suicide or the one who hints but will not answer questions, delighting to torture, pleased to have created a sensation, your temptation will be to get annoyed—especially if the teasing is a regular occurrence. Never allow yourself to say, "Well, go ahead and do it then!" They just may do that, without intending to die. People who play with death to get attention sometimes make mistakes. They miscalculate. It is therefore better to be safe than sorry, and in the case of a suicide tease to say, "You know, if you really want to commit suicide I may not be able to prevent you, even though I want to. But I don't want you to do it."

Many times I have been faced with patients who threaten me, "If you don't do what I ask, I shall kill myself. I mean it. I really will." With them I know I must make two things clear. First, I must never let myself be blackmailed by the threat of suicide. Yet at the same time I must tell my patient that the game is a dangerous one, that the responsibility for life is theirs as well as mine and that the last thing I want is to see my patient die.

Preventing Suicide

Only in Great Britain did the suicide rate fall steadily for a number of years. Why? What difference was there between Britain and other industrialized nations? Were emotional illnesses handled better there? Were suicide attempts treated more efficiently? Or were the Samaritans, a nonprofessional organization devoted to helping suicidal people, the key to the change? If so, is there an urgent need for suicide prevention centers to be set up in every Western city?

The attention of professionals was drawn to the efforts of the Samaritans in 1976 by Dr. C. R. Bagley.[2] Bagley compared the changes in suicide rates in 15 communities in Britain where Samaritan groups were established and functioning with 15 communities lacking them. Where Samaritan groups functioned, Bagley's calculations revealed a significant difference—a reduction in suicides.

The study awakened wide interest and heartened the Samaritans in their endeavors. Intrigued by its findings a Dr. B. M. Barraclough and his colleagues attempted to repeat the study using more rigorous methods. They included three more of the "Samaritan Cities" in their study and chose carefully matching communities for a comparison.[3] Disappointingly the team found no significant difference between the two sets of cities which had comparable suicide rates and suicide trends.

The complexities of such epidemiological studies are such that I hesitate to try to explain the difference in the findings of the two. Bagley in commenting on Barraclough's findings said as much: "I am of the opinion that the methodological difficulties of using the suicide rate to evaluate Samaritan efficiency are too great for any valid conclusions to be drawn.

Samaritans may be effective in reducing suicide to some extent, but there is no way of proving this."[4]

Yet British suicide rates fell. If the Samaritans did not account for the fall, what did? Psychiatrists would like to believe they are doing a better job treating mental illness, the incidence of which is clearly related to suicide. Emergency officers and ambulance drivers would like to feel that the fall results from more efficient rescue operations.

Unhappily, there is a much simpler cause—unhappily because it represents a factor which cannot readily be translated to other settings. Britain, like every nation, has its preferred mode of suicide. Britons had for generations committed suicide by putting their heads in the gas ovens in their kitchens and simply turning on the gas. The gas used to be coal gas, a gas with a high carbon monoxide content. Death is quiet and painless. Britons did use other methods of suicide, but few if any nations had as many "gas oven" suicides.

Alert to the danger of coal gas, the authorities reduced its carbon monoxide content till in 1971 it fell to less than 2%. Dr. James Brown reviewed the matter of British suicides in a 1974 article in *Archives of General Psychiatry*.[5] He pointed out that while successful suicides had decreased in Britain, the number of suicide attempts had risen at rates comparable with those in other countries. He also quoted a study by Kreitman.[6] Kreitman produced graphs to show that the fall in the suicide rate corresponded exactly to the period during which carbon monoxide was being progressively reduced from coal gas. He also showed that while deaths from coal-gas poisoning had dropped, the fall was partly offset by increased suicides by other means in all age groups. By 1976 the suicides by other means caused the overall rate to increase, as it continued to do through 1979. The tradition of putting one's head in the gas oven lingers on, although coal gas has now been completely replaced by much less toxic natural gas. We can hope that British suiciders will continue to try oven suicides and remain ignorant of its ineffectiveness till help arrives.

The British lesson may have value for us all. Certainly no harm will be done by operating suicide and crisis intervention centers, which already are springing up in North America and Europe. Many people contemplating suicide are lonely and desperate. A telephone conversation can mean the difference between life and death, at least for the time being. A friend who can offer companionship, a willing ear and suggestions of professional help may be the means of turning someone from death to life. Who should be more willing to reach out to the lonely and desperate than the church of Christ?

Britain's Samaritans and similar organizations may or may not reduce the number of suicides. But cutting out access to toxic substances will. In North America people do not commit suicide by breathing coal gas in their ovens, but they do swallow sleeping pills. The toxicity of sleeping pills varies enormously. Barbiturates are deadly and still widely prescribed. Modern sleeping pills related to the benzodiazepenes can be swallowed in great quantities with not nearly the same threat to life.

Of course, there are those of us who do our best not to prescribe sleeping pills at all. But it is unlikely that we will be able to persuade our hard-pressed colleagues in family practice to copy us. It is equally unlikely that health authorities will ever ban sleeping pills, though legislation *could* progressively phase out all barbiturate sleeping pills and any others that constitute a serious threat to life when swallowed in great quantity.

Antidepressant drugs are equally dangerous when taken in large quantities. Ironically the agent which may alleviate the depression may be swallowed by a half-cured patient in a moment of desperation, causing death instead of healing. Unfortunately, no effective nontoxic antidepressants yet exist. As for guns I can only shake my head in bewilderment. I know that the right to bear arms is championed throughout the West. As an Englishman I acknowledge either that I am myself insane or that North Americans are. The access to dangerous handguns in the Western Hemisphere to me amounts to criminal irresponsibility on the part of governments. For drugs and guns alike, the best we can hope for is careful screening of the suicide potential of every patient and the attempt to cut off every means of death in people judged still to be suicidal. No stone must be left unturned. Problem drinkers should be directed to Alcoholics Anonymous. Mental illness must be treated promptly. Legislation should subject toxic substances to tighter control. Christians should combat the tendency to large, impersonal churches, or at least encourage small groups capable of providing the intimate support suicidal patients need.

And we Christians must stop closing our eyes to suicide.

10
Straightening Bent Minds: Psychotherapies

Yea though I walk in death's dark
  vale
Yet will I fear no ill;
For Thou art with me, and Thy rod
And staff me comfort still.
Scottish Psalter 1650

At last the physicians, after a long
and stormy voyage, see land:
They have so good signs of the con-
coction of the disease, as they may
safely proceed to purge.
John Donne

Two books that have earned my admiration and respect more than any are those by D. Martyn Lloyd-Jones *(Spiritual Depression)* and the Puritan author William Bridge *(A Lifting Up for the Downcast)*. In September 1964 Lloyd-Jones wrote, "In several instances [concerning the relationship between the physical, the psychic, and the spiritual] I would have liked to deal with the problem more thoroughly." Lloyd-Jones made it clear that spiritual depression can have a physical cause. "Does someone hold the view that as long as you are a Christian it does not matter what the condition of your body is? . . . Temperament seems to some degree to be controlled by physical conditions."[1] Two things prevented Lloyd-Jones from pursuing this theme. One was that his book represents a series of sermons which seemed to him an inadequate medium for such complex matters. The other was that he intended the book to be not for "experts" but for "the common man."

I tremble to do what greater men of greater learning refrained from doing. Yet I have felt impelled to try. In doing so I must sound a note of warning. To read Bridge and Lloyd-Jones alone may cause us to assume something which neither author intended, that all depression is "spiritual" in the sense that bodily infirmity is never its source and that it has only "spiritual" remedies. To read my book with its emphasis on bodily processes may lead us to err in the opposite direction. I have therefore included some of the thoughts that Bridge and Lloyd-Jones emphasize.

I have also attempted that most difficult task of helping "the common man" to think more clearly about the relationship between our physical bodies and the nonphysical part of our beings. In doing so I have chosen to use the term *mind* in a broader sense than those biblical words translated "mind." I write as a psychiatrist as well as a Christian. Modern texts in the social sciences include aspects of our being (such as emotion and volition) that are not commonly included in the biblical words. My choice does not reflect a disrespect for Scripture so much as a desire to speak in a language we understand and to deal with the issue of Cartesian dualism and what is commonly termed the mind-body dichotomy—a dichotomy that leads to much confusion in the human sciences.

Throughout I have tried to be clear about two points. First, however significant may be the physical "causes" of our depressions, a grasp of Scripture, a hope in the God of Scripture and an awareness that we humans inhabit both a material and a physical world are of paramount importance. My second concern is that we be cautious of judgmental attitudes toward men and women struggling beneath the weight of depression, and of glib and inaccurate explanations of their condition. As I said earlier, the godliest men and women have been gripped by profound depression. David, Jeremiah,

Bunyan, Luther, Spurgeon and many others have been its victims. (Indeed, a book that is easy to read, Elizabeth Skoglund's *Coping,* consists precisely of a discussion of how Amy Carmichael, C. S. Lewis, Charles Spurgeon and Hudson Taylor dealt with emotional problems such as depression.) Even the Son of man once groaned, "My soul is very sorrowful, even to death," as he contemplated the cost of obedience to the father's will (Mk 14:34).

I have had another ambition in writing, and that is to reconcile the wide differences in viewpoint that characterize all mental illness. Since physicians, psychologists and counselors all earn bread by treating depression, it is understandable that verbal sniping and competitiveness should at times replace collaboration. Money, power and prestige are important to us all, however much we deny it, and those who are not medical professionals are understandably upset at the entrenched power of those who are. Even if money, power and prestige were to matter nothing to us, our experiences and the various indoctrinations we have undergone would produce differences in our views. Therefore, I do not pretend to be unbiased. Nevertheless I can assert that one of the great joys of my life is to watch drooping shoulders straighten, dull eyes begin to sparkle, weary limbs grow strong and laughter bubble from my depressed patients. Hardly a week goes by without my watching the miracle happen all over again. I thank God for my job. I can only trust that other professionals will excuse the biases.

Part of the problem lies in the fact that we see different populations of depressed people. I have never practiced psychiatry anywhere but on the wards and in the outpatient departments of hospitals, for three years at a provincial mental hospital and for thirteen years in the psychiatric departments of large teaching hospitals.

The depressed people I see include many who have been referred to me by other professionals or by relatives who perceived them to be in dire straits. Many if not most fall into the category of very sick patients. It is likely that the treatment they needed differs from those of depressed people others may see. If this is so, then the mix of treatments (psychotherapy, godly counseling, behavior therapy, antidepressants and electroconvulsive therapy) will include more pharmaceutical and mechanical components. Indeed I would suggest that the graver a particular depressive illness becomes and the more its pathophysiology is entrenched, the more important physical treatment grows. Other elements are certainly valuable as well. Human beings are not machines, and as helping persons we must be humble enough to learn from one another. Nevertheless, I believe that there is a rough spectrum in various depressions and that certain kinds of efforts will be more effective at one end of the spectrum than the other. The techniques we employ will overlap considerably—it is only right that they should—but none of them covers the spectrum alone.

More about Mind

Let me recapitulate some principles I discussed earlier.

Unless we grasp the essential character of human nature, we will have difficulty understanding "mental" illness. The model I have suggested, a model which conceives of mind as a group of bodily functions, does not seem to violate Scripture while it avoids the pitfalls of Cartesian dualism. No model does justice to the complex marvel of human nature. If my model is to be helpful, we must understand that traffic among body, brain and mind runs two ways. Again, if I am right, the approach to the treatment of mental disorder would seem at other times a combination. Current psychiatric practice seems to bear this out.

Our problem arises in part from having a mindset incapable of conceiving reality in any other than spacio-temporal terms. Try as we might we seem to be locked into such concepts. We find ourselves thinking of spirit, for example, as a sort of space-occupying entity, invisible, ghostlike, hovering somewhere within us. Our idea of mind may be even more vague, yet still space-occupying in some little understood fashion. If we can transcend dualistic thinking, however, and accept that bodily function is just as real as a physical body, it becomes easier to understand how psychological treatment can have physiological correlates and vice versa. Function is as much a reality as anatomy, just as music is as real as the symphonic score, the big difference being that the music cannot change the score whereas mind certainly can, by feedback, produce bodily changes.

This model raises a further question. Both Jewish and Christian Scriptures accept human immortality, in which we are not to be ephemeral and ghostly but to have bodily existence beyond the grave. I do not know whether death represents a temporary cessation of mind, but I suspect that the problem has to do with the relation between time and eternity. What I will affirm is that in the resurrection our bodies will be raised from the dead. Even more necessary to helping depressed people is an understanding both of the limitations and of the usefulness of science. Much that is written by Christians about depression represents pseudoscientific justification bolstering a personal theory about depression. Such writing is not truly biblical but an oversimplification or distortion of Scripture truth.

Let me then appeal to all of us who counsel, give dynamic therapy or administer medication to avoid closing our minds to concepts which threaten our theoretical positions. Let us be open-minded and humble, or we shall never grow in understanding. If we do not grow, our patients and clients will pay the price for our pride and our rigidity.

The treatment a depression calls for will vary according to its nature and severity. In its initial stages at least, depression is not one thing but several. We have enough evidence now to realize that the more serious a depression becomes, the more it will resemble any other depression as it converges with the "final common pathway." Like tributaries that arise hundreds of miles apart to converge in one great river, depressions differing widely at their sources become progressively more similar in their pathology. The more serious the depression, the better is its response to physical measures (antidepressant medication and ECT).

The first step in helping a depressed person will therefore consist of gaining as clear a view as possible of the nature and severity of that person's illness. Whatever style of interview is employed to examine the sufferer, detailed information must be obtained. The onset of the condition and its possible causes must be discussed. The symptoms and signs described in chapter five must be investigated. Suicidal ideas must be assessed. The presence or absence of hypothalamic signs must be determined, a family history explored, the patient's general health reviewed carefully and corroborative evidence sought from the sufferer's friends and relatives in the form of a collateral history. Depending on the picture that emerges from such an inquiry, a selection will be made from the remedies available.

Psychotherapy

Perhaps the most distinguished psychiatrist to champion the importance of psychotherapy is Silvano Arieti, a profoundly human and deeply respected teacher, writer and psychoanalyst with an international reputation. In 1978 he vigorously defended psychotherapy for profound depression, stating, "In over thirty years of clinical experience with depression, I have never seen a case about which I could say that there was no psychological factor involved"[2] and proceeded to describe what he saw as the fundamental psychological problem.

It is hard to categorize Arieti's position, which seems to

lie somewhere between classical psychoanalysis and cognitive therapy. Arieti feels that "the cognitive basis of the condition is repressed, but the painful feeling is very intensively experienced at the level of consciousness." He feels the therapist must avoid the traditional form of psychoanalysis; that is, of the patient lying on a couch and "freely associating." He must instead be firmly optimistic. The therapy will take time and consist in repeatedly going over the patient's life histories to relate the original "psychogenetic mechanisms" and "life patterns" with the way patients handle current problems.

Several things about Arieti's article bother me. I have the impression that it was written in response to a person he calls "a prominent psychiatrist and a leader in the fight against depression" (Nathan Kline, a fellow psychoanalyst) whose popular book stresses the importance of physiological mechanisms.[3] Arieti's article opens with his concern about Kline's views.

Again, while referring to his "thirty years' experience" with depression, he gives neither a statistical analysis nor even a description of one case. Instead he gives a complex explanation of the illness without any evidence to support his view and concludes by recommending "less frequent [therapy] sessions" (of between one and three times a week!) —a luxury only the rich could afford, especially since government-sponsored programs increasingly oppose such ideas on economic grounds. There are not enough therapists around to give each patient as much time as Arieti recommends. Arieti seems to retain the old dualism of body and mind, psyche and soma. He recognizes, however, the value of antidepressants and of ECT and sees no reason why they should not be combined with his form of psychotherapy. We will need more convincing arguments than Arieti provides if we are to accept his particular view of psychotherapy for depression.

Psychoanalytically oriented psychotherapy continues to be

the subject of careful research, however. A recent study attempted to find out whether it was possible to predict which patients would benefit from such psychotherapy.[4] Many of the 73 patients selected for the study showed "substantial gains" (though because there was no control group, it was not possible to say whether the gains were due to the therapy or merely due to the passage of time). The therapists, the patients, other clinical observers and data on other variables, however, all failed to predict which patients would improve. Among the patients were a few whose neurotic symptoms included feelings of depression.

While the exact role for the psychotherapy of depression is yet to be determined, certain principles already emerge. First, convincing evidence for therapy based on the Abraham-Freud view of retroflexed rage has never been demonstrated.

Second, the principal forms of psychotherapy that offer hope seem to be:

1. The mobilizing of grief in the depressed feelings (as distinct from depressive illness) following bereavement.

2. Some form of cognitive therapy.

3. Behavioral therapy designed to elicit nondepressive behavior.

4. Pastoral counseling.

5. Some physical form of treatment which, as a rule of thumb, is more likely to be required with the severer forms of depression, particularly those in which the victim's cognition (ability to think) is impaired. We will look at the first four forms of therapy in this chapter and the last form in chapter eleven.

Grief Work

Experienced therapists know from their contact with bereaved clients that some mild depressions can arise from unresolved grief. Remember, though, that unresolved grief is not the same as depressive illness. The Freud-Abraham view of depression is not entirely invalid, but relief to the sufferer comes not through mobilizing the patient's anger but through the patient's understanding that it is normal to feel resentment as well as love toward someone who has died.

We find it hard to let ourselves feel resentment to someone who has abandoned us by dying. To resent the dead is too shocking. Yet to recognize not only that anger is normal but also that it does not negate love can bring release. Some bereaved people are unable to mourn, either because they are afraid to discover resentment in themselves or because they consider grief to be a sign of weakness. They should be encouraged to remember times of happiness they enjoyed with the deceased as well as times of conflict. There is no place for locked-away memories following bereavement.

Grieving consists of remembering, of allowing oneself to remember and to sorrow over memories that meant much to us. It consists of coming to terms with reality, the reality that the person who died was human and had weaknesses, yet had endearing traits that were precious and which are sorely missed. It consists of realizing, little by little, that one chapter in life is over. It is a chapter that can be reviewed from time to time but that belongs essentially to the past, for a new chapter of life is beginning. We cannot begin a new chapter without having dealt thoroughly with the past.

Some bereaved people feel that they are to blame for the death of someone they love. They may be right or wrong about their belief, but their anxiety and guilt hinder normal, healthy grieving. Usually they experience relief by merely sharing their fear and sense of guilt and discussing it with a sympathetic listener.

A few people will lock up the bedroom of the deceased person. They do not want to face the pain of going through clothing, books and personal possessions that are charged with painful memories. Yet to do so is essential for "grief work" will not be complete until this is carried out. I recommend that a close friend or a counselor do this with the bereaved person, usually the day following the funeral.

We have already seen that the symptoms of normal grief (episodic sighing, weeping, a loss of interest in other things) can be expected to last up to two or three months.[5] We have also seen that some people, because of either heredity or bereavements in early childhood, are high risks for major depressive illness with subsequent bereavements.[6] Such people need more help with their task of grieving.

Most of us would probably prefer either to give or to receive help by psychotherapy than by medication. To be able with the therapist's help to grapple with wrong habits of thought, to find the power to overthrow distorted views with accurate ones seems more consonant with human rationality and dignity than to have our chemistry tampered with. It makes us uneasy to think that we are dependent on the electrochemical functioning of our brains and that we are not altogether in control of our destinies. Nevertheless, we must face the constraints of reality. We must not sacrifice clients and patients on the altar of our ideology. There are illnesses in which sufferers have no access to reality. Words lose their content. The only reality they can perceive is the false reality their disordered brains produce for them.

In a recent study[7] 81 depressed patients were diagnosed as suffering from either endogenous (or biological forms of) depressions or else reactive depressions (those with circumstantial causes). They were randomly assigned to three treatment groups. In one group they received interpersonal psychotherapy. In the second group they received a tricyclic antidepressant. Members of the third group of patients were given both treatments. Both kinds of patients (reactive and endogenous) were found in all three groups. The results showed that both kinds of patients responded to the combined therapy. The endogenous patients, however, did not respond to psychotherapy alone, whereas the reactive pa-

tients responded equally well to either antidepressants or
interpersonal psychotherapy.

It would seem that it is not possible to separate endogenous
from reactive depressions in advance. Time and money also
place limits on psychotherapy. There never will be enough
trained therapists to help even those sufferers who can benefit
from and afford their help.

Cognitive Therapy

George Kelly,[8] Albert Ellis,[9] and Aaron Beck[10] have all been
exponents of what Beck calls cognitive therapy, which I discussed earlier in chapter six. There are some differences
between their views, but their underlying assumptions and
purpose are the same. I shall therefore choose to discuss
Beck's views since they are more widely known and perhaps
backed by better and more recent studies than those of the
other authors. To my mind the most lucid description of cognitive therapy is one by Rush and Beck.[11] Cognitive therapy
arises from a trilogy of concepts: a cognitive triad, schemas
and cognitive errors.

The cognitive triad, as mentioned earlier, consists of a
negative view of oneself, negative interpretations of one's
experiences and a negative view of the future. First, such
patients blame and criticize themselves. Next, they interpret
all that happens to them in a negative way even in the face
of more plausible explanations. For instance, a perfunctory
greeting from a husband who is under great financial stress
may be interpreted by his depressed wife to mean that she
is too unattractive to be loved. Third, they perceive the future
as hopeless.

The concept of schemas may be a little harder to grasp. It
too involves our interpretation of what is happening around
us. We weave such things as sights, sounds, smells and the
actions of people in our lives into a picture we call reality. A
moment ago we noted the tendency of depressed patients

to place negative interpretation on their ongoing experiences. Schemas refer to our habitual ways of interpreting events and responding to them, and account for why you might see a set of events differently from me. They are "stable cognitive patterns," the individually tinted spectacles through which we each view reality.

Beck's third concept, cognitive errors, are errors in logic affecting the sufferer's interpretation of events, such as:

arbitrary inferences—conclusions for which no grounds exist;

selective abstraction—focusing on a negative element in the picture rather than positive elements;

overgeneralization—drawing general conclusions from a single incident;

magnification and minimization—magnifying negative elements and minimizing positive elements so as to seriously distort the picture of reality; and

personalization—feeling that the words or actions of other people are motivated by hostility to yourself.

Cognitive therapy is short-term, time-limited psychotherapy of up to twenty sessions over a ten- to twelve-week period. To an outsider such as myself, the essence of the treatment seems to lie in a sensitive but Socratic probing of patients' experiences to enable them to discover the logical errors associated with their depressions and the false schemas that underlie their views of themselves and their everyday lives.

A therapist will try to get patients to express their thoughts about specific upsetting events ("What did you think about her telephoning you like that?") and look at possible distortions in the evaluations by getting them to examine all the evidence. Then the therapist will be on the lookout for habitual patterns of evaluation (schemas) and teach the patient to recognize them and even to anticipate them. Finally, the therapist teaches the patient to identify the specific logical errors listed above.

The therapist will also tackle specific problems (suicidal wishes, inactivity, self-criticism) and give the patient homework in the form of instructions for ways to tackle target symptoms. The tasks will be graded carefully so as not to overwhelm patients but rather to let them experience the gratification of triumphing, however small the triumph.

Cognitive therapy has strong points in its favor. But Beck is wrong in believing it is the ultimate weapon against depression and is trying to extend it beyond its natural limitations. Depression has an uncanny way of overthrowing cognition, and I have watched half-amused, half-saddened by the perplexed expressions on the faces of some of my more insightful patients whose depressions return. They begin to describe their feelings of guilt, of unworthiness or whatever, then stop, look at me and say, "I know what you're going to say. You're going to tell me that I am thinking like this *because I'm depressed.* And I am depressed. But I really feel I *was* being irresponsible and that I *am* a total failure." Our grasp of reality is tenuous at the best of times. Cognition bows very readily to other "realities" which can quickly engulf us.

Workers like Beck and Ellis are simplistic in their assumption that what I think determines how I feel. It is just as true to say that how I feel determines what I think. Let me but suffer simultaneously from headaches and arthritis, and hills will swell to mountains. In such a condition "reality" eludes cognition.

Moreover, serious moral problems are raised. Is sin only sin because I believe it to be so? Is my sense of guilt *always* an artifact of depression? Supposing among my schemata is one that tells me that my neglect of my family offends a holy God. Which needs correction: my schema or my attitude toward my family?

And how would Beck or Ellis cope with the drive to suicide that so often accompanies demonization? Are demons subject to logic?

Kant and Cognitive Therapy

Jerome Yesavage[12] recently pointed out interesting parallels between eighteenth- and nineteenth-century philosophies and the modern controversy over cognitive therapy. The philosopher Immanuel Kant lived at a time when philosophers based their ideas (as cognitive therapists do) either on *reason* or on *experience*. Descartes, whom I discussed earlier, stressed reason. His basic premise was *cogito ergo sum*—I think; therefore, I must exist. His understanding of human nature and of the universe arose from this proposition. Other philosophers suggested that experience, our sensory experience of the world around us, formed the basis of true knowledge. Locke, for example (who is thought to have greatly influenced the Puritan theologian Jonathan Edwards), insisted that knowledge was based on experience. The two reigning schools (rationalism and empiricism) gave the foundation on which modern physics and chemistry have been built. Their view of human beings is also remarkably similar to that of cognitive therapists. Beck, Ellis and Kelly are really bedfellows of Descartes, Leibnitz, Locke and Hume.

Against this cold intellectualism of rationalist empiricism, the romantics passionately sought other ways of discovering truth. Musicians, poets and novelists sought truth intuitively, feeling it to be a matter of heart rather than head. Many of us who are Christians, while being neither rationalist-empiricists nor romantics, have been aware of truths which baffle our minds but bring unspeakable joy to our hearts.

> How thou canst love me as I am
> And be the God thou art
> Is darkness to my intellect
> But sunshine to my heart.
>   (Unknown)

Kant was profoundly influenced by Rousseau and avidly read the romantics. In his famous *Critique of Pure Reason* he attempted to discover the place and relative value of rationalist empiricism and romanticism. To Kant there seemed no sound basis for supposing that cognition (or logic) was a more reliable guide to truth than our emotional impulses.

In a sense, Kant tells us that we can never really know anything for sure. The "real things" around us—desks, chairs, books, plants are undoubtedly *there,* so to speak, but we do not *know* them. We merely organize the sensations of light and color that come to us from them and formulate categories in our minds. Their essential character eludes us. Even the "realities" of time, space and causality are ways in which our minds interpret our experiences. Kant insisted that "the thing in itself," the noumena, the true essence of something (a flower, for example), always eludes our cognitive faculties. We see the surface of reality as we organize our own perceptions (phenomena.)

In the same way we cannot truly know ourselves (the "self-in-itself") but only our experience of selfhood. Nevertheless, we seem to enjoy a certain degree of independence and may also be immortal. "By opening the possibility of free action and immortality in the noumenal world alongside a scientific phenomenal world, Kant balances his romantic and cognitive beliefs."[13]

The strengths and weaknesses of cognitive psychotherapy are the strengths and weaknesses of rationalist-empiricism, as Kant saw them. Our expectations, assumptions and perceptions of the world around us powerfully shape our behavior and our future experiences. What we see (whether or not we see correctly) determines what happens to us. Neither an optimist nor a pessimist may see life as it is, yet the optimist will generally get along better in life than the pessimist and the two will certainly behave differently. This is why cognitive therapy can be so effective. To the extent that depressed patients can be helped to perceive life differently and to have different expectations, their depressions will lift.

Still, corresponding weaknesses exist in cognitive therapy. It can no more serve as an infallible guide to reality than rationalist empiricism can because of the danger of extending it beyond its proper limits. Albert Ellis recognizes the limits of reason[14] but continues to defend reason, whatever its limitations, as the only guide we have. Kant distrusted human judgment, based as it is on human concepts and human experience—both of them subjective. For this reason he believed the noumenal world of ethics and religion is of "practical" help in guiding our everyday lives.

Interestingly, modern brain research suggests a physical basis for Kant's views. One hemisphere of our brains (usually the left) interprets our experiences, codifying and storing them in symbols and words and sorting them out so that we make rational decisions. The other hemisphere seems to operate in what we might loosely call intuitive ways, being concerned with analogical, creative and artistic thinking. We thus possess two complementary organs of thought each operating on quite different principles. If we are indeed created by God, this fact suggests that the organs are meant to complement each other and that both ways of thinking are valuable for us and for his purposes.

Behavior Therapy

Behaviorists are less interested in what goes on in "the black box" of the mind than in depressive behaviors. Depressive behaviors, however, include not only the way patients behave (including psychomotor retardation, and sleep and appetite disturbances) but also patients' "verbal output," what they say about how they feel. Behavior therapy will aim to extinguish depressive behaviors (that is, to stop patients from moping around and saying how bad they feel) by not reinforcing such behaviors (in popular terms, by ignoring them) and by reinforcing nondepressive behaviors. Alternately, they might "punish depressive behaviors via aversive conditioning, an unpleasant reaction from the environment elicited by depressive behaviors. In their review of behavioral treatment Liberman and Raskin quote a number of attempts by behaviorists to treat depression.[15] Lazarus, treating reactive depressions, employed three techniques:[16]

1. He instructed patients to imagine themselves advancing in time and engaging in enjoyable activities and relationships.

2. He encouraged the patient to produce nondepressive behavior.

3. He induced "sensory deprivation" to "sensitize" patients to incoming stimuli, especially to positive reinforcement of desirable behavior. An example of sensory deprivation is that of prolonged sleep, used by Korita therapy developed in Japan[17] by which patients are given absolute bed rest for about one week.

The application of some form of behavioral techniques can be demanding. It requires stringent and detailed examination of environmental stimuli that elicit depressive behavior in a particular patient, and a detailed list of behaviors to be extinguished and to be elicited. For hospitalized depressed patients there must be rigorous training of the ward staff who must consistently give or withhold the specific reinforcements each patient needs. Because it is demanding of staff time, it is therefore expensive. Although there is good evidence of its effectiveness, especially with milder forms of depression, there is as yet little evidence of its effectiveness in deep depressive illness.

Moreover, the underlying philosophy of behaviorism presents the Christian with problems. It assumes that human beings are closed systems incapable of spontaneous behavior and totally subject to reconditioning.

Pastoral Counseling

Pastoral counseling for depression has a long and checkered history. Medieval counselors saw "accidie" (depression) as a sin to be fled. Frank Lake quotes ancient records about a certain Saint Seraphim who "commanded us to fear above all things, and to flee as we would from the fire, the chief of sins, accidie. . . . There is no worse sin, my mother, and nothing more terrifying and destructive than the spirit of accidie." He evidently recommended eating bread to cure it.[18] Had the good saint observed that the sin of accidie made people lose weight?

I would like to think of pastoral counseling as spiritual counsel, applying biblical teaching to spiritual needs in the counselee. I grow uneasy at the tendency of some seminaries to collaborate with the psychology or human behavior departments of secular universities. I say this not because secular institutions have nothing to teach us. My whole education has been either secular or else (in high school) in a setting of old-fashioned liberal theology. I perceive, however, a tendency among men and women whose higher education has been basically in Christian institutions to be too fascinated by the psychologies and particularly by some of the more faddish pop psychologies of the day. Ministers can benefit from some understanding of psychology and psychiatry. Their most valuable contribution though will always be to minister Christ and his Word, and to deal with sin, the world, the flesh and the devil, where these are the true causes of the counselee's distress.

It is not always easy to know when depression is mainly a spiritual matter. In the case of the patient I described in the opening chapter, it seemed clear that understanding the grace of God was enough to change a paranoid and profoundly depressed man into a joyful and liberated one. Among the thousands of patients I have treated, however, he is the only seriously depressed person whose psychological needs were met by spiritual understanding. More frequently I see spiritual understanding restored by psychiatric treatment. I know of no simple rule of thumb by which what

Lloyd-Jones calls spiritual depression can be distinguished from one caused by stress, disrupted affectional bonds, genetic vulnerability or physiological imbalances. I suspect that the boundaries between the two are loose and shifting.

All we can do is listen as the sufferers explain their feelings and gently explore every possible factor involved. If the prayerful administration of God's truth fails to benefit sufferers, ministers should not necessarily blame themselves nor accuse those they counsel of stubbornness or unbelief. Perhaps some aspects of the problem call for the skills and insights of a psychologist or a physician.

One area that seems to be of special importance in pastoral counseling is the crippling sense of guilt arising from an inadequate grasp of the grace of God in the face of Satanic accusations (see Rev 12:10-11). Much evangelical teaching renders Christians peculiarly vulnerable to it. No one ever says so explicitly but most evangelicals, I am convinced, unconsciously assume that God's loving acceptance of them depends on their postconversion spiritual performance rather than on the perfect sacrifice on their behalf by the Son of man. They know the theory of justification but derive no spiritual succor from it. It is impossible to exaggerate the crippling paralysis caused by an inadequate understanding of God's justifying grace.

A second area where the pastoral counselor can offer help, whatever the root cause of the depression, is to teach and to encourage the sufferers (provided they have enough ability to concentrate) in solid, inductive Bible study, and to discourage mere devotional reading. In most depressed people devotional reading has either stopped altogether, or it has degenerated into something unhealthy and unhelpful.

Years ago, when I was seriously depressed, the thing that saved my own sanity was a dry-as-dust grappling with Hosea's prophecy. I spent weeks, morning by morning, making meticulous notes, checking historical allusions in the text. Slowly I began to sense the ground under my feet growing steadily firmer. I knew without any doubt that healing was constantly springing from my struggle to grasp the meaning of the prophecy.

Third, when dealing with patients with serious depressive illness, pastoral counselors must realize that such people are helplessly in the grip of something they cannot control. Any method used to help them will take time, sometimes many weeks. Yet such patients are not entirely helpless. There is at least one freedom that remains, the freedom to choose what posture they will adopt to their painful experience.

Often I read the third chapter of the book of Lamentations to such patients. Whether Aaron Beck is right or wrong about the centrality of hopelessness, hope is something that is almost always possible. The crux of Lamentations 3 is the poet's refusal to relinquish hope in God.

Paul reminds us of the importance of the triad: faith, hope and love. We hear much about faith and love. The only connotation of hope in modern preaching seems to be eschatological. Yet hope is precisely what distressed people need. It is the forward-looking equivalent of faith, faith in what God will do eventually because of who he is and because his mercies are daily renewed. I therefore take my seriously depressed patients to biblical passages written by profoundly depressed people (it is always a comfort to know that "people in the Bible" were sometimes cast down) and insist that as long as God is true to his name, hope is possible.

The best attitude of seriously depressed people is to quit struggling for instant happiness and to hope and quietly wait for the Lord. By this I do not mean that they must be passive or that they must avoid medical or psychological intervention, but their progress will be faster and their anxiety greatly relieved if they can grasp that hoping and waiting quietly for God's time are vital to the battle. In our present state of knowledge the proverb, "More haste, less speed," applies to the counseling of depressed people.

The Scriptures have much to say about "waiting upon the Lord." Many different Hebrew words are translated by the English word *hope*. Some have the connotation of silence or stillness (Ps 62:1, 5; 65:1). Others imply an active choice to await a response (Job 32:4, Ps 33:20; 106:13; Is 8:17). One word, *yachal*, means specifically to wait expectantly or to wait with hope. Indeed the word is translated "hope" more frequently than "wait" (Job 14:14 and Ps 33:20 as "wait," and Ps 33:18 as "hope"). Translations seem to differ as to whether *yachal* should be translated "hope" or "wait" in different contexts (Job 6:11 RSV and KJV).

Waiting hopefully, expectantly and with quiet endurance forms a theme both of the Old Testament and the New. Indeed a good preparation for anyone engaged in counseling would be to do word studies on Greek and Hebrew words translated "hope" and "wait" in English. We have forgotten the importance of such an idea in our age of instant, ready-made solutions. Because I have never heard a sermon on hope, I presume that our preaching may reflect our cultural bent toward instant solutions.

My fourth recommendation is that we lend or give to people who could benefit from them either of two books I mentioned earlier: Lloyd-Jones's *Spiritual Depression: Its Causes and Cure* or William Bridges' *A Lifting Up for the Downcast*, both of which are essential reading for the would-be pastoral counselor.

Finally, what should pastoral counselors do when their efforts fail to improve matters? I must repeat my suggestion that they be slow to blame the counselee, and that if after a month or so discouragement persists, counselors should suspect that other ministrations may be called for and refer the counselee either to a family doctor or to a competent psychologist or psychiatrist.

11
Straightening Bent Minds: Physical Therapies

Diseases, which we never felt in ourselves, come but to a compassion of others that have endured them; nay, compassion itself comes to no great degree, if we have not felt in some proportion in ourselves that which we lament and condole in another. But when we have had those torments in their exaltation, ourselves, we tremble at relapse.

John Donne, Devotions xxiii

For years the scientific literature has been swollen with articles describing the effects of antidepressants, both tricyclic antidepressants (TCAs) and monoamine oxidase inhibitors MAOIs). Although the articles vary in quality, evidence for the effectiveness of antidepressants is now overwhelming. As the quality of scientific studies improves, the effectiveness of these medications grows more firmly entrenched. Later in this chapter we shall compare their effectiveness with electroconvulsive therapy, just as in a previous chapter we considered their mode of operation. In doing the latter we laid the foundations for answering Judge Joseph Tauro's charge that to use medications against patients' wishes is to violate the rights of such patients by using "powerful and mind altering drugs" for "involuntary mind control."

Antidepressants are used to help patients whose brain

biochemistry is already crippling their ability to perceive reality and subjecting them to fears and psychic pain. Antidepressants are mind-straightening drugs. Powerful they may be. But far from controlling the minds of depressed patients the medications *restore to depressed people a control that has been impaired.* They are not happiness pills. They have nothing in common with medications such as Valium. They cannot produce euphoria. They do not produce a high (except in some bipolar patients in whom they precipitate a manic phase and in whom they must be used with great caution). No one is tempted to take them as an escape, for they provide none. Because of their mild side effects (which I will describe later) they are not particularly pleasant to take and some people who need them have to be encouraged to continue to use them. Their beneficial effects are not instantaneous and they may require weeks before they achieve their full effects.

Since 1971 researchers have endeavored to discover why some antidepressants seem more effective than others, and why the same dose of an antidepressant will restore one patient to health but will fail to do so in another patient of the same size, sex, weight and depth of depression.

Tricyclic Antidepressants (TCAs)

Increasing attention has been devoted to the relation between the dose of TCA and the blood levels of their active ingredients. More research is needed, but already it is clear that the response to the medications is related to these blood levels rather than to dosage. Thus one patient on 150 mg of imipramine will have a higher blood level and a better response than another patient who is taking the same dose of the same TCA. Two of the commonest TCAs are imipramine (original trade name, Tofranil) and amitriptyline (original trade name, Elavil). It now seems clear that their effectiveness increases according to their blood levels until they reach 650 nanograms per milliliter of blood.[1] Unfortunately, a dose will not necessarily produce the same blood levels in different patients, though there seems to be general agreement that doses of less than 150 to 200 mgs daily will not usually achieve effective blood levels. The use of alcohol, tobacco, oral contraceptives, barbiturates and other sleeping pills may impair the results of even these doses.[2] The picture is more confusing with other TCAs, for some studies are marred by methodological flaws. I eagerly await the day when correct dosages of anti-depressant medications can be monitored by blood levels.

In the meantime my custom with depressed patients to whom I give antidepressants is to spend time explaining all we know about their method of operation, their side effects and the delay before their benefits are felt. I also encourage patients to take the medication in a single dose in the evening. In this way patients experience fewer of the side effects and are less likely to forget to take their medication in the busy rush of the day. This may explain why patients get better more quickly on a once-a-day schedule than patients taking medication three times daily.[3]

Side effects include a dry mouth, constipation, an increased pulse rate and increased sweating. All are mild and patients are glad to put up with them once they have experienced the benefits of the medication. Some patients also experience what is known as orthostatic hypotension, a feeling of faintness when they get up too quickly from sitting or lying down. (Some people experience this when they are on no medication.) Rapid adjustments are required when we stand so that our blood pressure remains roughly the same. These adjustments may be slightly delayed under the influence of TCAs. The problem is easily overcome by promptly sitting down again and getting up more slowly.

The most worrisome side effect is a slight slowing of the conductivity of heart nerves and muscles. In patients under fifty this is not a great concern, but in people over fifty or people who already suffer from heart disease, it is best to choose those TCAs which have the least effect on heart muscle.[4]

Monoamine Oxidase Inhibitors (MAOIs)

As I mentioned in an earlier chapter MAOIs, though less effective than TCAs, have a role in the treatment of depression, though the descriptions of the patients who respond best to them are hardly flattering. A type of depression named hysteroid dysphoria was described in 1969 by psychiatrists Klein and Davis.[5] It occurs in women whose mood is shallow and labile, and who are histrionic, flamboyant and seductive. The authors insist, however, that these features arise from the depression and disappear when it is treated. Other workers who presented a paper at an American Psychiatric Association convention confirmed the diagnosis and its response to MAOIs. They added three more characteristics of responsive patients: "rejection sensitivity, applause-hunger and a craving for sweets."[6]

People taking MAOIs must watch their diets carefully to exclude certain elements which react with the drug to produce catastrophic rises in blood pressure and extremely severe headaches. Most physicians hand their patients a list of things to be avoided—such items as aged cheeses, certain red wines and antihistamines.

For a long time it was considered dangerous to mix TCAs and MAOIs. The fear is now known to be unfounded. Provided certain precautions are followed, the two types of antidepressants can be used simultaneously in depressions that resist other forms of treatment. They constitute an extremely potent antidepressant combination.

People sometimes ask me whether Valium is an antidepressant and if so, of what type. Valium belongs to a group of drugs called minor tranquilizers. It alleviates anxiety temporarily. It has no effect on depression, and my personal practice is never to use minor tranquilizers if I can possibly avoid doing so.

Lithium

Lithium is one of the most important discoveries in the treatment of mood illnesses. Its value in treating bipolar illness is hard to exaggerate. The U.S. National Institute of Mental Health recently estimated that the use of the salt in the United States between 1969 and 1979 resulted in a $2.88 billion drop in the cost of treatment and a $1.28 billion gain in increased productivity, a saving of more than $4 billion.[7]

Earlier I described the nature and action of lithium but said little about how it can be used. Physicians vary in their practice. In manic patients I begin with a dose of 300 mg three times daily, monitoring blood levels three times weekly. I increase the dose slowly until the blood levels stabilize in the therapeutic range (between 0.8 and 1.2 mgs per 100 mls of blood). Lithium can irritate the lining of the stomach and is best taken during or immediately after a meal. It can produce a fine tremor which is exaggerated when the patient is self-conscious or nervous. Drinking coffee and signing checks can become a problem. But again, the benefits outweigh the disadvantages.

Unfortunately, lithium can reduce the activity of the thyroid gland if it is used for long periods. In patients who use it all their lives, regular checks must be made on thyroid function, and thyroid supplements may be necessary. Lithium also affects kidney function, reducing the kidney's ability to filter impurities and concentrate them in urine. So far as we can tell this effect is completely reversible. Functions all return to normal after a brief "lithium holiday."[8]

If a patient has several attacks of mania, the question of lifelong lithium use arises. The subject is a controversial one, especially because higher doses of lithium can be seriously toxic, producing vomiting, diarrhea and delirium. To my mind, however, the advantages outweigh the risks.

More controversial is the use of lithium to treat depression.[9] At this writing, the Food and Drug Administration and a task force appointed by the American Psychiatric Association do not recommend its use in depression.

Gradually our sophistication in using the many medications available to us is increasing. We are better able to predict on the basis of a patient's history and certain biochemical tests which patients will do best on which medications. In the meantime a second generation of antidepressant drugs (nomifensine, trazadone, zimelidine and mianserin) is now undergoing clinical trials around the world. Although at the time of writing they are only used in research trials in North America, soon they should be readily available.

Why do we need more medications? Is the present variety inadequate? Why spend millions of dollars in research merely to multiply the variety of available antidepressants? Are the new drugs more potent than the old?

So far as we can judge from the few reports available, the potency of the new drugs is similar to those already in use. They are attractive because of their fewer side effects and because some may reduce the possibility of future depressions. One of them, nomifensine, seems at this point to have no toxic effects on the heart—a very real concern in older patients or those with existing heart disease.

Electroconvulsive Therapy (ECT)

Let me now broach the controversial subject of "shock treatments," as they are popularly called, or electroconvulsive therapy (ECT) as its advocates prefer to call it. ECT consists of administering a series of small electrical shocks to the brain in order to induce convulsions. Seen by its opponents as a brutal exploitation of helpless victims by punitive psychiatrists who know nothing about how ECT works, it is touted by its advocates as an enlightened, humane measure about which a great deal is now known. The truth lies somewhere between the two extremes, though to my mind nearer the view of its advocates than that of its enemies.

ECT has unquestionably been misused widely, particularly

in the period immediately following World War 2. At that time state and provincial hospitals were overpopulated and understaffed. Mentally ill patients and the staff who cared for them represented the Cinderellas of medicine, nursing and psychology. The staffs of large mental hospitals were often inadequately trained, underpaid and expected to care for too many patients. Sometimes control was a more burning issue than treatment, so that patients were often overmedicated, and ECT was used to treat conditions in which it had little value.

Where did ECT come from? What was the idea behind it?

In 1935 Ladislaus Meduna hit on the idea of treating schizophrenia by inducing epileptic seizures. Meduna had made the erroneous observation that people with schizophrenia never suffered from epilepsy. On this false premise he argued that schizophrenia might be eliminated if schizophrenics were made to convulse. Initial reports of convulsive treatment were enthusiastic. Various methods of inducing seizures were used such as injections of camphor and other convulsion-producing drugs. In 1938 Ugo Cerletti and L. Bini replaced drugs with electricity and "shock treatment" was born.

The treatment came at the time when very little could be done to help severely ill patients crowding large mental institutions, so that the staffs were ready to clutch at anything that might help. Various uses of ECT were promoted including REST (regressive electroshock therapy). REST consisted of giving numerous treatments to schizophrenic patients who then "regressed" to a childlike state characterized by confusion and incontinence of bowel and bladder. The idea behind REST was kindly. Theorists suggested that by making patients children again and by giving them a "corrective experience" of being reared anew with love and nurturing support, their schizophrenia would disappear. But the theory did not work.

Inevitably ECT was widely misused in desperate efforts

to help "hopeless" cases, and mental health organizations began to protest against its inhumanity. In public demonstrations pig brains were fried to illustrate the damage ECT allegedly caused to human brains. Because of opposition, careful studies were carried out by both advocates and opponents of the method so that slowly, over the years, its exact effects, its method of operation and its true sphere of usefulness have emerged. Popular myths, however, die hard as do understandable fears, and ECT is still regarded with suspicion and apprehension. Films like *One Flew over the Cuckoo's Nest*, mentioned earlier, have done nothing to allay public apprehension and have only added to the fears of some desperately needy patients. The film, a clever and moving representation of conditions existing thirty years ago (but largely abolished today), merely served to entrench public superstitions about ECT. Dramatic horror makes a better box office than does truth.

Is ECT effective? How does it work?

Effective it most certainly is, provided its use is limited to certain conditions, of which depressive illness is the most important. Freeman, in a 1979 article in the *British Journal of Hospital Medicine* that is one of the best summaries about ECT, states, "ECT is not a treatment for unhappiness. It cannot mend marriages or restore to the bereaved their relatives. However, it is an effective treatment for severe depressive illness or endogenous depressions, that is, those characterized by sleep disturbance, loss of appetite and weight, retardation, a morbid sense of guilt, and sometimes paranoid, nihilistic and somatic delusions. In fact in these conditions it appears to be the most effective and rapidly acting treatment available."[10]

Seven studies reported in the English language on more than 2,000 patients clearly showed that ECT was more effective than antidepressant medication.[11] Most of them were written before modern forms of ECT were widely used. The latest study is summarized as follows:

> Seventy-two consecutive patients treated with electrocon-
> vulsive therapy (ECT) for severe mental illness were asked
> their opinions about ECT: 83% considered they had im-
> proved as a result of the treatment and 81%would have it
> again. Most found the experience neutral or pleasant and
> 54% thought the dentist more distressing. Claims in news-
> papers, magazines, television and elsewhere that ECT is
> cruel and frightening receive little support from the results
> of the study.[12]

Modern ECT bears little resemblance to ECT in the 1930s
and 40s. Nowadays it is more humane and more scientific.
It is largely limited to treating conditions we know will benefit
from it. Patients who undergo it will be given a short-acting
intravenous anesthetic (so that they will be unconscious before
ECT is administered) together with muscle relaxants (so that
the seizure will cause a minimum of bodily movement). Special precautions are also taken to cut down memory loss. Atro-
pine is administered to keep pulse and blood pressure low.

It is unfortunate that negative findings about ECT receive
more publicity than careful studies about its true value. For
instance, an article in *Biological Psychiatry* was widely quoted as
evidence of the uselessness of ECT. It described how a Dr.
J. E. Jones discovered that for a period of time he had been
administering ECT to patients with a machine that was internally disconnected—apparently to Jones's satisfaction. But as
Barton[13] pointed out, Jones documented no assessment of
the outcome of his studies, and should not have been allowed
to give them for so long without supervision. Moreover,
Jones seemed to confuse side effects of the treatment with
its benefits. We are revising our ideas on placebo effects.

The fact is that ECT, used appropriately, has proved itself
repeatedly to be lifesaving. But what of its advantages and
disadvantages? And why does it work?

In 1978 careful and prolonged experiments were carried

out on the effect of ECT on rats.[14] Among these effects were the enhancement of transmissions across the synapses between nerves. Grahame-Smith and his colleagues discovered that these beneficial results could only be obtained if several treatments were given. Moreover, the treatments had to be spaced—at intervals of one or two days. Several treatments in one day were less effective than the same number of treatments over several days. They also discovered that the effects could be produced equally well by what is known as unilateral ECT (current applied to only one side of the brain but producing seizure activity in both brain hemispheres) as by bilateral ECT, but that a bilateral convulsion had to occur if the improved neurotransmissions were to take place. Finally, they discovered that it did not matter how the convulsion was produced. The effects of the convulsions were the critical factor. A number of studies have also compared unilateral with bilateral ECT in human beings.[15]

ECT's benefits have nothing to do with electricity nor with the methods by which convulsions are produced. The biological consequences of convulsions (a release of neurotransmitters) lead to the improvement. The longer each convulsion lasts, the more pronounced is the curative effect of ECT.

The most unpleasant side effect of ECT, as I have already indicated, is memory loss, retrograde (of things before the treatment) and anterograde (of things occurring immediately following treatment). Studies on memory loss give conflicting results.

Unquestionably the greatest memory loss will concern events immediately surrounding the period of treatment. It affects some patients but leaves others with intact memories. Patients sometimes complain that they have lost older memories—of telephone numbers, events or names of friends. In a careful study comparing memory before and six to nine months after treatment, Squire and Chase,[16] applying six different kinds of test, could find no evidence of delayed retention or persisting memory impairment. Nevertheless, several of the patients in the test reported memory loss. The authors suggested that the discrepancy could mean either that the tests were not sensitive enough to detect the memory loss or else that the ECT had drawn to the patient's attention memories that they had previously lost.

How can the unpleasant loss of memory be reduced?

First, it must be realized that memory impairment depends on two factors, the amount of current affecting the brain and the position of the electrodes on the head. Newer machines which apply smaller quantities of electricity (some in bursts of 1/2000 second repeated over about 5 seconds) produce less memory loss. Stimulation applied to only one side of the brain can also reduce memory loss.

To understand this, more should be said about the two halves of the brain. The two hemispheres lie side by side like mirror images. In infancy their functions are interchangeable. In fact one hemisphere could be removed from an infant brain without any impairment to the infant's growth or intelligence. But as life advances each hemisphere develops specific functions. The dominant hemisphere governs verbal functions, including speech and verbal memories. For most people (whether they are right-or left-handed) the left hemisphere is dominant. If ECT electrodes are placed over the non-dominant hemisphere (usually the right), the benefits of the treatment are just as pronounced while the side effects (loss of memory and posttreatment headache) are greatly decreased and sometimes nonexistent.[17]

Controversy about ECT centered for a while over a study known as the Italian De Carolis study. Only available in English in the form of an abbreviated synopsis, the synopsis gravely distorted De Carolis's findings, suggesting that ECT was ineffective. In the De Carolis study high doses of imipramine (a tricyclic antidepressant) were compared with electroconvulsive therapy. The study is one of the only studies in which high doses of antidepressant were compared with ECT. De Carolis demonstrated that ECT was more effective than imipramine both in depressed patients as a whole and, more importantly, in patients with the most severe depressions.[18]

The debate about the superiority of ECT over antidepressant drugs continues. Slowly we are coming to realize that ECT is faster and somewhat safer than antidepressants. It is more effective in women than in men. Memory impairment and headaches remain disadvantages, especially when the electrodes are placed on both sides of the head.[19] It is not without risk, even risk to life, though the task force appointed by the American Psychiatric Association found that death occurred "extremely rarely."[20] Indeed ECT is much safer either than leaving the depression untreated or than treating depression with tricyclic antidepressants.

In a study published in 1976 Avery and Winokur followed the progress of 519 depressed patients, some treated with ECT, others with "adequate" antidepressant and yet others (in a younger age group) with no treatment. During three years the number of deaths (mostly from coronary artery disease, cancer, strokes and suicide) was significantly less in the group treated with ECT. In the group taking antidepressant medication the death rate was less (though not to a "statistically significant" degree) than in the untreated group.[21] The same two workers re-examined their data and in 1978 published a study of suicide attempts occurring in the 519 patients during the first six months after treatment. In the ECT group the rate was 0.8%. In patients on higher doses of antidepressant medication, the attempted suicide rate was 4.2%, while among those taking smaller but "adequate" doses of antidepressant medication, it rose to 7.0%.[22]

Depressive illness can kill. The two commonest causes of death appear to be from coronary artery disease and suicide. It is puzzling to find that death from cancer, from heart disease and from cerebrovascular accidents (strokes) is significantly less in depressed patients treated with ECT than in those treated with antidepressants. We can only assume that depression may indeed lower the body's resistance to disease or that antidepressants increase the chances of coronary artery disease. At any rate it is now clear that the much feared "shock treatment" administered under modern conditions is the safest and most effective treatment for serious depression.

It is particularly valuable in the treatment of elderly patients in whom confusion is commonly attributed to senility. Among confused elderly people are a number whose confusion arises from undiagnosed depression.[23]

Among the "senile" patients admitted to the hospital under my care during the last twelve months I can recall three, aged 86, 82 and 79, all suffering from "confusion" and "dementia." Two had serious heart problems and one could not swallow. After very careful medical and psychiatric work-ups, all three appeared to be suffering from serious depressive illness. In consultation with internists and anesthesiologists, we decided that ECT would be the safest and most humane treatment. Two are still living independently and caring for themselves. Their "senility" has evaporated. One lived until a couple of months ago in a nursing home where the staff "couldn't get over" how alert and happy she had become. I must not give the impression that all confused elderly people are depressed. On the other hand, some confusion in elderly patients *is* depressive and responds well to ECT.

The debate rages over whether ECT should be forced on an unwilling patient. I will not at this point discuss the complex ethical issues involved. The law in Manitoba gives me the right to force treatment on patients "where there is danger to the patient or to other people." In the few instances where I have obliged patients to undergo ECT, I have been moved by the response of formerly suicidal patients. Always they have told me that they were glad that I interfered with their attempts to kill themselves.

The literature on ECT is now voluminous and it would be impossible to review it all here. Perhaps the most interesting way to conclude this section would be to quote extensively from a 1965 article written by a British psychiatrist who himself had undergone ECT.[24]

I am a practising psychiatrist who has had the personal experience of receiving two series of treatments of ECT for depression in different hospitals as an out-patient. I had one series of three treatments three years ago, and I have only just finished another series of five treatments.

It might be useful to describe the subjective experience of the treatment as far as possible in objective terms, because there seems to be much groundless fear of ECT. I have heard fellow psychiatrists decry this form of treatment as a brutal attack upon the person, and I have known them to withhold it from patients to whom no doubt it would have brought great relief, or in whose case it might have even been a life-saving measure. From my personal experience of having the treatment and from my experience of giving ECT to patients as a psychiatrist, I know it to be a highly effective treatment in depressions of endogenous or non-reactive type, with the great advantage that some measure of relief nearly always becomes immediately apparent.

With the modern technique of adequate anesthesia and relaxant drugs the patient loses consciousness pleasantly and quickly and is aware of nothing until he wakes up in the recovery room. For the next couple of hours he feels a little unsteady and ataxic; in the second series of treatments, though not in the first, I have felt nausea after treatment, and on two occasions I have vomitted after reaching home by car. I have not been able to discover whether the difference in technique at the two hospitals or some other difference was responsible for this nausea during the second course of treatment.

Another mildly unpleasant sensation which I have had

after the first treatment in both series is a stiffness of the jaw, which lasted about a day. This evidently is a common experience after the initial treatment, but does not recur after subsequent treatments in the series.

One of the most celebrated effects of ECT is the memory loss it induces. This can be alarming, as whole tracts of memory seem to be expunged without trace. Memory for recent events, during the week or so preceding treatment, appears to be the most severely affected. Memories for events of several years ago seem to be impaired hardly at all. The way in which memory returns is very interesting. When an event, entirely forgotten, is brought to one's notice, it sounds completely strange, foreign and unknown. One has the feeling that a confabulation is being presented: the details of the account seem unnecessarily elaborate, as if to make the story convincing, and the whole effect is almost laughable. Then a fragment of the story rings true; a name is recognized, for example, and a series of events or facts come suddenly to mind, in a linear sequence, as one element leads to the next. The revelation has a marked quality of unreality, as if one is trying to convince oneself of something fictitious, and as one gropes one's way along the sequence it is as if one is looking at the remembered facts for the very first time. This feeling of alienation is very strong, even in the face of indisputable evidence of the reality of the remembered facts. It is as though one can synthesize the fragmented elements of memory in this way. Although it is a strange experience, it is in some ways quite delightful. It is as if one is seeing at least some aspects of life through new eyes. One might speculate that the fragmentation of imagery and the opportunity it affords for resynthesis in this way may be one of the therapeutic benefits conferred by ECT. . . .

I am writing this only five days after my last treatment, and there are still many gaps in my memory, though I am confident that these will close. Meanwhile I find the process of resynthesis from fragments a source of amusement. I am no longer sad and tearful. Every day I am feeling more energetic and I look forward hopefully to a marked positive improvement in spirits in a few weeks' time if events follow the same course as last time.

I hope that this account will help to dispel the erroneous belief that ECT is a terrifying form of treatment, crippling in its effects on the memory and in other ways. The technique is today so refined that the patient suffers a minimum of discomfort, and the therapeutic benefits are so great in those cases where it is indicated that it is a great pity to withhold it from mistaken ideas of kindness to the patient.

Combined Help

Let me conclude this chapter by discussing my own practice and problems. At the beginning of the book I hope I made it clear that depression is not one thing, qualitatively or quantitatively, but many. It can be a mood, a malady or a madness. As research in many areas continues I am overwhelmed by the journals that continue to pour into my office. In some ways issues are sharpening and clarifying. In other ways new knowledge seems to make matters more confusing than ever.

Yet of one thing I remain convinced. Human beings are whole beings, and so long as I continue to practice psychiatry I must treat them as such. I will no more treat mind as distinct from body than body as distinct from mind. By the grace of God I will treat persons, not pathology, sinners rather than syndromes and individuals rather than illnesses. I must treat the person rather than mind, brain, central nervous system, body. And however primitive our weapons may be, there are effective weapons and we must use them.

The problem is always to treat the whole person without anyone else's help. I believe I can examine patients well, use appropriate tests and come to reasonable conclusions as to the nature of the problem. But to treat the suffering person may demand skills beyond those I possess.

I can and do administer medications and ECT where they are called for. I can and do spend time with patients, especially in the earlier more critical phases of their illness, helping them to understand what is happening, listening to their doubts and fears, meeting with the members of their family whose own anxieties and even hostility I may need to overcome.

At times I work along cognitive lines, for while cognitive therapists are mistaken in claiming for their system an all-encompassing effectiveness, it has value. Function can affect matter, or mind affect body.

As for the bewildering array of new findings I am forced to be selective in what I study. I recognize not only that I am limited in what I learn and practice, but that I am part of a team whose members contribute a variety of skills needed by different patients to differing degrees. I am not yet satisfied about the contribution of behavioral science to depressive illness, but I still will consult a behavioral psychologist where I think his expertise may be of value.

I also collaborate with pastoral and other counselors. Shortage of time and a heavy schedule often hinder me from spending as much time as I would like with my depressed patients, and I may work with a counselor, my own role being more medical, while the counselor or pastor may see my patient more frequently and deal with spiritual or psychological issues. Clearly such collaboration calls for clear communication between me and my coworker.

My misgivings about the training of pastoral counselors must not be taken to mean I see no need for pastoral ministry to depressed patients. Rather I feel that the wrong kind of information has often been taught them, a kind that relies too heavily on the fake science of pop psychology (the pseudo-profundities of transactional analysis, the games theories of Eric Berne, the mystique of the Gestalt, the slickness of

Thomas Harris and the obscenities of Alex Comfort). Before they embark on any clinical counseling I wish that all would-be pastoral counselors would read, mark, learn and inwardly digest *Psychology as Religion* by Paul C. Vitz, a devastating commentary on the state of psychological therapies being used today.

Christian psychiatrists need pastors as our greatest allies. Yet, too often pastors want to dump undesirable members of their congregations into our laps, saying, "Here, doctor. You take over." Some patients enrage me by calling my office saying, "Pastor X says I've got to make an appointment with you." Yet pastors and psychiatrists both have contributions to make in dealing with depressive illness.

I pray that this book may mark a new beginning in such collaboration.

Epilog:
Pain & Shame
Which Should Not Exist

I have two final concerns: one for people under psychiatric care and the other for counselors who care for them. Both illustrate the needless pain and shame of depressive illness.

The Social Lepers

Among the patients who came to my office this week were two evangelical Christians who had suffered major depressions. Both had recovered well but were still on medication. The first, a married woman in her midthirties, had been hurt by attitudes displayed to her by members of her church on her return from the hospital. Among other reactions was one by the Sunday-school superintendent. Without my patient's knowledge he had arranged for a younger and inexperienced woman to assist her in taking a Sunday-school class she had taught for years and which (she felt) she had always handled competently. When she approached the Sunday-school superintendent to ask the reason for the change, she was told, "Well, we knew you had not been well, so we thought that with someone else to help you, you would not be under so much strain." (In fact, she was now under more because the assistant had opposing ideas about how the class should be conducted.)

The superintendent's reaction was understandable but blameworthy. "I wouldn't have felt so badly if he had spoken to me first. He seemed so embarrassed that I felt I was some kind of leper. When I was sick they did nothing, but now I am well they do *this*." She may have been overreacting. If so, both her own and the superintendent's reactions stem from a common cause, *the shame and disgrace associated with having psychiatric treatment,* especially for depression which "no Christians ought to have."

My second patient was a man in his fifties who had experienced severe depressions for ten months of every year during the preceding seven years. His exceptional competence had enabled him to hold his job in spite of a performance which was far below his best. During his most recent depression he had contemplated suicide. "But I would find it very hard to talk about it to the church. . . . It's too fresh in my mind." Yet as he spoke he knew he was thoroughly well and delighted at being so. Again his reaction springs from the taboo surrounding depression and suicide in Christian circles.

The taboo is widespread. One church council decided that they would have to relieve a church officer of her duties "because we understand she's on some kind of psychiatric medication." (She was taking antidepressant medication.) The issue was not one of her suitability but of her medication. Little did the council know that the secretary who recorded their minutes (who happened to be my patient) was on the same medication. The secretary's reaction can be imagined. To whom could she turn for understanding if the leadership of the church had such an attitude? Would she also be fired if the council knew of her condition?

The taboo has two causes. In the first place we are afraid, somewhat dishonest and therefore unkind to psychiatric patients. We do in fact treat them "like social lepers." Our fears are not excusable, especially when such patients are fellow Christians. I know that some psychiatric patients behave in a bizarre manner and can be socially embarrassing. But when depressively ill patients are made well, they are perfectly normal.

In addition to our unkindness we are ignorant, ignorant of the nature of depressive illness and of the greatly improved outlook for seriously depressed patients. How will Christ judge us in a coming day? He sat down with a prostitute at one point in his life and talked to her about her salvation, much to the embarrassment of his disciples. He was despised by the religious people of his day for consorting "with publicans and sinners." He was a physician who saw his business as being among the sick, and the "sick" were usually those people whom the religious and respectable shunned and still shun, with many others who Jesus loves—alcoholics, the sexually sinful and others who are emotionally disturbed. We avoid them. We prefer to send them to an expert of some kind and hope that will be the end of the matter. If we should be so unfortunate as to bump into them, we joke about it to our friends or else are embarrassed.

But my patients see through the whole thing. They are as aware of the taboos and rejections as those who are more fortunate. I tell them, "It doesn't matter how your brothers and sisters in Christ behave. Christ himself understands. He has not abandoned you." But what conclusion do my patients draw from what I say? The only conclusion they can draw is that Christ is very different from most Christians. And they are right.

In this book I have also discussed the hurtful self-condemnation that other depressively ill people endure because of the "have-more-faith-give-yourself-a-kick-in-the-pants" attitudes they may encounter. Such attitudes are appropriate to those who are not ill but are burdened with care or else are self-pitying. They are not appropriate for the sick. Indeed they have done and still are doing incalculable harm.

Depressed Counselors

Now for my second concern. Psychiatrists get depressed. So do counselors, psychologists and pastors. Pastors, I feel, are as much at risk for serious depression as psychiatrists. Tragically, when people who are accustomed to their role as helpers get depressed they experience more difficulty than the average person in seeking professional help and in making good use of it when they find it.

Again, it is a matter of needless shame and pain. It is said that doctors and nurses make the worst patients. Pastoral counselors, psychologists and psychiatrists also make bad patients and clients. They combine shame at being unable to cope with the shame of becoming dependent on a colleague.

It is essential that the depressed counselor seek help promptly. I can think of few things more pathetic than a profoundly depressed counselor listening to a profoundly depressed client. Depressed counselors find themselves at sea. They need to be resilient and confident to counsel well. While they must always resist the temptation to jump to conclusions, they have to be able to make serious decisions and sometimes quick ones. But when our thinking is slowed, our morale and our confidence in ourselves low, we become too indecisive to help anyone. It is true that good counseling consists more of listening than of talking, but it is far from true that the counselor should be a passive agent, swept along by the depressed flow of the client's thoughts. Therefore counselors should themselves both seek help when they are depressed and trust the judgments of the persons they seek out. If they fail to do so, they may have fallen into the trap of believing their role to be that of the omnipotent, omniscient guide of the weak.

But there is a prior difficulty. Counselors (particularly pastoral counselors and pastors) are often the last ones to recognize what is happening. Most depressed Christians blame themselves for their feelings but no one so frequently as the pastor.

There are reasons for this. Pastors who counsel (like Christians generally) see their weariness, their reluctance to pray and to read Scripture as spiritual problems which of course they can be. But sometimes the real problem is the onset of depressive illness.

Pastors are forced to be an example to their flock. As they dry up emotionally, and experience heaviness and weariness, sermon preparation can become a chore and visitation something to shrink from. "What kind of a pastor am I when I don't feel any love for the members of my congregation? When I don't have any message to give them? When I am a poor father and husband? When I'm lazy and wish I could get out of the ministry?"

The Christian environment adds (I am sorry to say) to their difficulties. If a pastor makes a tentative approach to sharing his difficulties with a friend, he may meet with anything from breezy clichés to books on the horrors of spiritual warfare, books which damn him as defeated and call on him to grapple with dark foes.

Both the cliché and the book on spiritual warfare have a valid place in Christian experience. The critical issue concerns the pastors' or counselors' true condition. Are they merely overworked or perhaps in need of watching and prayer? Do they need a holiday? Or are they psychiatrically ill?

I offer one piece of advice to anyone who feels they may be in such straits. Seek help. Seek it from a competent professional. There is help somewhere for you. Find it. God has not forsaken you. In his grace he has, somewhere, someone who can help you, who can alleviate your distress.

My object in writing has been solely to relieve the pain of depressive illness by making Christians more aware of what it is and how it can be helped. I want to join hands with physicians, psychologists, pastors, counselors of every variety and the enlightened Christian public in doing battle with this common plague, so frequently made worse and more painful by the misguided attempts to help that some Christians make.

So if you are yourself depressed, get help. It may be that your distress is the first step in your being able to help others in similar difficulties. And if you are not depressed, but are fighting in the same battle with me, I want to encourage you and to add my small contribution to the sum of your own understanding as you deal with depressed people.

So let us join hands. The task ahead is long and arduous, but having God with us, we need not fear the outcome.

Glossary

A

Activism   the tendency to exalt faith to a point where it becomes a means of forcing God's hand; in contrast to Quietism.

adrenergic system   a nerve network whose function depends on adrenalin, a neurotransmitter.

affect   sustained mood; affect is to mood what climate is to weather.

affective illness   mood illness or mental illnesses which are associated basically with disorders of mood.

agitated depression   see *depression, agitated*.

altruistic suicide   see *suicide, altruistic*.

amitriptyline   the generic name of a widely used and inexpensive TCA.

anaclitic depression   see *depression, anaclitic*.

anhedonia   the inability to experience pleasure.

anomic suicide   see *suicide, anomic*.

attachment bonds   emotional ties to another person.

aversive conditioning a term from behavioral psychology referring to the process of producing a change in someone's behavior by linking a particular piece of behavior with something unpleasant—an aversive stimulus.

axon an insulated elongation of a neuron, carrying impulses to other neurons.

B

bipolar depression see *depression, bipolar.*

bonding the process by which attachment bonds are formed.

C

cholinergic system a nerve network whose function depends on acetyl choline.

circadian rhythms body rhythms governed by the earth's rotation.

clinical psychologists see *psychologists, clinical.*

clustering a statistical device aimed at simplifying complex data.

cognition rational, logical thinking.

cognitive errors errors in the observation and interpretation of facts.

cognitive set attitude, mental outlook.

cognitive triad a group of mental functions considered by Aaron Beck and his colleagues to be basic causes of depression and its treatment.

collateral history additional information supplied by a patient's relatives or friends.

compulsions something the victim has to do in order to relieve his or her anxiety; e.g., checking three times to be quite sure the stove is turned off. The compulsion is irresistible, even though the victim might see it as ridiculous.

conscious that part of the mind which has to do with awareness.

correlates two or more processes which occur simultaneously or in close succession, but that are not necessarily explained casually.

cortisol a chemical belonging to the steroid group related to bodily stress. Cortisol is increased in some forms of depression.

D

demonization   a New Testament word often translated by expressions such as "possessed by an unclean spirit."

dendrites   nerve cell filaments collecting impulses from other nerve cells.

depression, agitated   a depression in which the victim gives way to endless worries, preoccupations and futile activities.

depression, anaclitic   an often fatal depression in bereaved infants.

depression, bipolar   a form of depressive illness in which there are "highs" (hyperactive and euphoric states) as well as "lows" (depressions).

depression, endogenous   depression once thought to be caused solely by bodily (endogenous) factors.

depression, manic   an illness which manifests opposites, "highs" (or bouts of mania) and "lows" (or bouts of depression).

depression, primary   depressive illness that is not associated with any other physical illness or "psychological condition" such as alcoholism, homosexuality or schizophrenia.

depression, reactive   depression once thought to arise purely because of outward (exogenous) factors.

depression, secondary   depression which arises in the course of another physical or mental illness.

depressive   speech, behavior or symptoms associated with depression.

depressive illness   prolonged change in mood, concentration, appetite, sleep and/or sexual patterns, associated with underlying changes in the electrochemical function of the brain.

Diagnostic and Statistical Manual of Mental Disorders   an attempt by the American Psychiatric Association to classify mental illnesses and to give detailed criteria for their diagnosis.

diurnal mood variation   mood that varies in response to the time of day, usually being worse in the morning but relieved in the evening.

DSM III   see *Diagnostic and Statistical Manual of Mental Disorders.*

dysphoric mood   an unpleasant or disagreeable mood.

E

ECT   electroconvulsive therapy, sometimes misnamed "shock" treatment.

ego   a Freudian term referring to that part of the mind which deals with reality and which negotiates with id and superego in their struggle to dominate our behavior.

ego ideal   what one consciously aims to be or become.

ego states   psychological conditions of which the subject is aware.

egoistic suicide   see *suicide, egoistic.*

Elavil   the original trade name for amitriptyline.

empathic   having empathy, the ability to "tune in" to someone else's feelings and experiences.

endogenous depression   see *depression, endogenous*

epilepsy   an illness characterized by seizures and usually controllable by medication.

epileptiform   movements or activity that resemble epilepsy.

exorcism   a word commonly used to mean the process by which unclean spirits are "cast out" of a demonized victim.

F

factor analysis   one of many statistical techniques used to evaluate the results of a study.

final common pathway   a set of symptoms and signs which several illnesses may share in common once they are advanced enough.

fugue state   a condition of intense emotional stress in which the subject seems unable to speak and may seem unaware of and unresponsive to his or her surroundings. Usually the appearance is deceptive in that hearing, vision and memory are actively functioning.

G

go system   a nerve network linked with the pleasure area of the brain.

grief   the mood that commonly accompanies the death of a loved person or the loss of something of overriding importance.

H

hypothalamic symptoms   symptoms arising from malfunction of the hypothalamus.

hypothalamus   a nerve center in the brain which regulates appetite, weight, sexual drive, sleep and other bodily functions.

hysteroid dysphoria   a depressive syndrome, more common in women than in men, where depressed feelings occur in association with "hysterical" behavior.

I

id   a Freudian term for those primitive instincts which we confine largely to the unconsciousness, particularly our sexual and aggressive drives.

id psychology   Freudian psychology which attached great significance to the largely unconscious id drives.

imipramine   the generic name of the commonest TCA.

L

lithium   a metal usually found in the form of a salt (e.g., lithium carbonate) and used in the treatment of bipolar affective illness.

logotherapy   a form of psychotherapy invented by Victor Frankl which concerns itself with the meaning of a client's life.

M

mania   a period of excitement and exaltation involving excessive speech and activity, impaired judgment and sometimes loss of contact with reality.

manic depression   see *depression, manic.*

MAOI   see *monoamine oxidase inhibitor.*

melancholia   an old term for depressive illness.

233

mitochondria minute body inside cells which manufactures molecules for a variety of purposes.

monoamine oxidase inhibitor (MAOI) an antidepressant that blocks the action of monoamine oxidase, an enzyme that destroys certain neurotransmitters.

mood-congruent "fitting in" with a mood; e.g., to have the delusion that one is bankrupt when the delusion arises from a depressive illness is a mood-congruent delusion.

N

narcissistic injury a blow to one's self-love.

neuron a nerve cell.

neurotransmitters complex molecules that conduct electrical impulses across the synapse separating one neuron from another.

noogenic neurosis a widespread emotional discomfort which arises, according to Victor Frankl, from the absence of meaning in human lives today.

noumena Kant's term for the real essence of something, a reality which always eludes us—"the thing in itself."

O

object someone or something to whom or to which we become attached by loving bonds.

objective having actual existence; uninfluenced by emotion or personal prejudice.

obsessions repetitive preoccupations; e.g., tunes which play themselves endlessly in the mind, or worries (often unreasonable worries) of which the victims cannot rid themselves.

orthostatic hypotension a temporary fall in blood pressure following a change in posture.

P

phenomena that which can be observed.

phobias fears, either general or specific; e.g., snake phobia—a fear of snakes, claustrophobias—fears of enclosed spaces.

pituitary gland a cluster of nerve cells under the control of the hypothalamus; the pituitary gland releases hormones influencing a variety of bodily functions.

placebo effect once thought to be a psychological effect in which, say, patients would feel better because they believed they were taking a powerful drug whereas the "drug" was not a drug at all. Recent studies indicate that the belief operates by releasing morphinelike substances in the brain.

possession a word used to translate the N.T. word *demonized*, referring to demonic control of a victim.

primal parathymia a term used by Karl Abraham to describe the susceptibility of a bereaved child to depression later in life.

primary depression see *depression, primary*.

psychiatrist a physician who treats mental illness.

psychologist one who studies varieties of human behavior.

psychologist, clinical a psychologist who measures human attributes and conditions, and treats illnesses.

psychomotor retardation a slowing up of speech, thought and behavior, observed in some forms of depressive illness.

psychosis a mental illness in which the victim has lost touch with reality and misinterprets what is seen and heard.

punishment area a nerve center in the brain governing frightening and unpleasant experiences.

Q

Quietism a religious movement led by Miguel de Molinos, emphasizing the principles of passive acceptance of all that happens to us as coming from God and designed for our perfection.

R

reactive depression see *depression, reactive*

reinforcement a behavioral term explaining the establishment of a habit by means of instantly rewarding an action and thereby encouraging its repetition.

REST regressive electroshock treatments now no longer used, in which an excessive number of treatments was used to "regress" patients to an infantile state, as a prelude to a "corrective experience" of love and care.

retroflexed rage   anger which, instead of being directed at the real cause of the anger, is directed inwardly at oneself.

reward area   a nerve center in the brain governing pleasurable experiences.

S

schemas   characteristic thought patterns of an individual that may contribute to depression. Part of the *cognitive triad* of supposed mechanisms.

schizo affective   an illness in which a mood disorder and schizophorialike symptoms are blended.

schizophrenia   a single illness or else a group of illnesses (at this time we cannot tell) characterized by episodes of insanity and by a progressive destruction of the schizophrenic's personality and deterioration of his or her ability to function in society.

secondary depression   see *depression, secondary*

seizure   a fit or attack in which subjects temporarily lose control of certain body movements, often with a loss of consciousness and occasionally with a loss of bowel and bladder control.

sociologist   one who studies the laws that govern the behavior and reactions of human beings in social interaction.

stop system   a nerve network linked to the brain's punishment center.

subjective   inner experiences, feelings, impressions not necessarily affected by the external world. Fear, for example, is something one may experience subjectively while another may not, though both persons are in the same circumstances.

suicide, altruistic   Emil Durkheim's term for suicides benefiting the society of the victim.

suicide, anomic   Emil Durkheim's term for suicides that are associated with changes in one's social circumstances.

suicide, egoistic   Emil Durkheim's term for suicides associated with some degree of psychosocial independence.

superego   roughly equivalent in Freudian thought to the

biblical idea of conscience.

symbolic possessions   nonmaterial acquisitions such as power, admiration, prestige.

T

TCA   tricyclic antidepressants.

Tofranil   the original trade name of imipramine.

transient situational reactions   short-lived emotional upsets in response to difficult circumstances.

tricyclic antidepressant   a medication (whose molecular structure includes three benzene rings) that is effective in treating depressive illness; TCA.

U

unconscious   that part of the mind in Freudian theory of whose activity we are unaware, but which may nevertheless exert a powerful influence on our behavior.

unipolar depression   an illness in which there are only "lows" and no "highs" (or manic periods).

Notes

Chapter 1
[1] Sigmund Freud, "Mourning and Melancholia," in *General Psychological Theory*, vol. 5 of *Sigmund Freud: Collected Papers*, ed. Philip Riett (New York: Collier, 1917), p. 164.

Chapter 2
[1] Kurt Koch, *Occult Bondage and Deliverance* (Grand Rapids, Mich.: Kregel Publications, 1971), p. 75.
[2] Ibid., p. 154.
[3] Ibid., p. 155.
[4] William P. Wilson, "Hysteria and Demons, Depression and Oppression, Good and Evil"; Basil Jackson, "Reflections on the Demonic: A Psychiatric Perspective"; John White, "Problems and Procedures in Exorcism"; *Demon Possession,* ed. John W. Montgomery (Minneapolis: Bethany Fellowship, 1976); pp. 223-31, 256-67, 281-99.

Chapter 3
[1] C. Adam and P. Tanner, *Works of Descartes,* 8 vols. (Paris: 1897-1913), 7: 203; as quoted in Frederick Copleston, *A History of Philosophy,* 9 vols. (Garden City, N.Y.: Image Books, 1962), 4:130-32.
[2] Adam and Tanner, *Works of Descartes,* 11: 351-52.
[3] Ibid., pp. 334-35.
[4] F. G. Alexander and S. T. Selesnick, *The History of Psychiatry* (New Yor Harper & Row, 1966), p. 3.

[5]R. C. Upham, *The Life of Madame Guyon* (London: Allenson & Co. Ltd., 1905), p. 136.

Chapter 4

[1]T. Holmes and R. H. Rahe, "The Social Readjustment Scale," *Journal of Psychosomatic Medicine* 11 (1967): 213.

[2]E. Paykel et al., "Life Events and Depression," *Archives of General Psychiatry* 21 (1970): 753-60 (hereafter cited as *Archives*); K. Thompson and H. Hendrie, "Environmental Stress in Primary Depressive Illness," *Archives* 26 (1972): 130-32; R. Kendall and J. Gourlay, "The Clinical Distinction between Psychotic and Neurotic Depressions," *British Journal of Psychiatry* 117 (1970): 257-66 (hereafter cited as *Brit. Journ. of Psych.*).

[3]Quoted in W. Fiske, *Measuring the Concepts of Personality* (Hawthorne, N.Y.: Aldine Publishing Co., 1971), p. ix.

[4]Aaron T. Beck, *Depression: Causes and Treatment* (Philadelphia: Univ. of Pennsylvania Press, 1967), pp. 175-76, 338-39.

[5]W. K. Zung, "From Art to Science, The Diagnosis & Treatment of Depression," *Archives* 29 (1973): 328-37.

[6]M. Hamilton, "A Rating Scale for Depression," *Journal of Neurology, Neurosurgery & Psychiatry* 23 (1960): 56-62.

[7]R. Schnurr, P. C. S. Koaken and F. J. Jarrett, "Comparison of Depression Inventories in a Clinical Population," *Canadian Psychiatric Association Journal* 21 (1976): 473-76 (hereafter cited as *Canadian Psychiatric*).

Chapter 5

[1]H. S. Akiskal and W. T. McKinney, "Overview of Recent Research in Depression: Integration of Ten Conceptual Models into a Comprehensive Clinical Frame," *Archives* 32 (1975): 285-305.

[2]Quoted in *Abnormal Psychology*, ed. Max Hamilton (New York: Penguin Books, 1967), pp. 66-69.

[3]M. Scarf, "The Promiscuous Woman," *Psychology Today*, July 1980, pp. 78-87.

[4]G. Carlson and M. Strober, "Affective Disorder in Adolescents" in "Affective Disorders: Special Clinical Forms," ed. H. S. Akiskal, *Psychiatric Clinics of North America* 12, No. 3 (December 1979): 509-26 (hereafter cited as *Psychiatric Clinics*).

[5]D. V. Sheehan, J. Ballenger and G. Jacobsen, "Treatment of Endogenous Anxiety with Phobic, Hysterical, and Hypochondriacal Symptoms," *Archives* 37 (1980): 51-59.

[6]R. C. Bowen and J. Kohout, "The Relationship between Agoraphobia and Primary Affective Disorders," *Canadian Psychiatric* 24 (1979): 317-22.

[7]H. S. Akiskal et al., "Psychotic Forms of Depression and Mania," *Psychiatric Clinics* 12, No. 3 (December 1979): 419-39.

[8]Emil Kraepelin, "Manic-Depressive Insanity and Paranoia," *Abnormal Psychology*, p. 75.

[9]D. Blumer et al., "Systematic Treatment of Chronic Pain with Anti-depressants," awaiting publication (1980).

[10]A. Rifkin et al., "Lithium Carbonate in Emotionally Unstable Character Disorder," *Archives* 27 (1972): 519-23.

[11]B. Herzberg and C. Coppen, "Changes in Psychological Symptoms in Women Taking Oral Contraceptives," *Brit. Journ. of Psych.* 116 (1970): 161-64.

[12]E. M. Brooke, "National Statistics on the Epidemiology of Mental Illness," *Journal of Mental Science* 105 (1959): 893; R. E. Hemphill, "The Incidence and Nature of Puerperal Mental Illness," *British Medical Journal* 2 (1952): 1232 (hereafter cited as *Brit. Med. Journ.*); P. Lomas, "The Husband-Wife Relationship in Cases of Puerperal Breakdown," *British Journal of Medical Psychology* 32 (1959): 117 (hereafter cited as *BJMP*); id., "Defensive Organization and Puerperal Breakdown," *BJMP* 33 (1960): 61; id., "Dread of Envy as an Aetiological Factor in Puerperal Breakdown," ibid., p. 105.

[13]M. Sim, "Abortion and the Psychiatrist," *Brit. Med. Journ.* 2 (1963): 145.

[14]B. Pitt, "Atypical Depression Following Childbirth," *Brit. Journ. of Psych.* 114 (1968): 1325-35.

[15]A. Munro, "Psychiatric Illness in Gynaecological Outpatients: A Preliminary Study," *Brit. Journ. of Psych.* 115 (1969): 807-09; E. Stengel, B. B. Zeitlin and E. H. Raynor, "The Post-Operative Psychoses," *Journal of Mental Science* 104 (1958): 389-410; M. G. Barker, "Psychiatric Illness after Hysterectomy," *Brit. Med. Journ.* 2 (1968): 91-95; D. H. Richards, "Depression after Hysterectomy," *Lancet* 2 (1973): 430-32.

[16]C. B. Bellinger, "Psychiatric Symptoms in Pre-Menopausal Women," *Brit. Journ. of Psych.* 131 (1977): 83-89.

[17]J. O. Cavenar, Jr., A. A. Maltbie and L. Austin, "Depression Simulating Organic Brain Disease," *American Journal of Psychiatry* 136, No. 4 (1979) (hereafter cited as *Amer. Journ. of Psych.*).

[18]American Psychiatric Association, Committee on Nomenclature and Statistics, *Diagnostic and Statistical Manual of Mental Disorders,* 3rd ed. (Washington D.C.: American Psychiatric Association, 1980).

[19]T. A. Ramsey et al., "The Erythrocyte/Lithium-Plasma/Lithium Ratio in Patients with Primary Affective Disorder," *Archives* 36 (1979): 457-61.

[20]M. G. Allan, "Twin Studies of Affective Illness," *Archives* 33 (1976): 1476-78; J. Angst and C. Perris, "The Nosology of Endogenous Depression: Comparison of the Results of Two Studies," *International Journal of Mental Health* 1 (1972): 145-58.

[21]R. Cadoret and G. Winokur, "Genetic Studies of Affective Disorders," *Nature and Treatment of Depression,* ed. F. F. Flach and S. C. Draghi (New York: John Wiley & Sons, 1975), pp. 335-46; T. Rich and G. Winokur, "Family History Studies V: The Genetics of Mania," *Amer. Journ. of*

Psych. 125 (1969): 1358-69.

[22]G. A. Carlson and F. K. Goodwin, "The Stages of Mania: A Longitudinal Analysis of the Manic Episode," *Archives* 28 (1973): 221-27.

Chapter 6

[1]H. S. Akiskal and W. T. McKinney, "Overview of Recent Research in Depression: Integration of Ten Conceptual Models into a Comprehensive Clinical Frame," *Archives* 32 (1975): 285-305; id., "Depressive Disorders: Toward a Unified Hypothesis," *Science* 182 (October 1974): 20-29.

[2]Akiskal and McKinney, "Overview."

[3]K. Abraham, "Notes on the Psychoanalytic Investigation and Treatment of Manic Depressive Insanity and Allied Conditions," *Selected Papers*, ed. E. Jones (London: Hogarth Press, 1927), pp. 137-56.

[4]Freud, "Mourning and Melancholia," p. 165.

[5]Ibid., p. 169.

[6]Ibid., p. 174.

[7]Ibid., p. 165.

[8]K. Abraham, "A Short Study of the Development of the Libido Viewed in the Light of Mental Disorders," *On Character and Libido Development* (New York: W. W. Norton & Co., 1966), pp. 67-150.

[9]Akiskal and McKinney, "Overview."

[10]Harry Harlow, "The Nature of Love," *American Psychologist* 13 (1958): 673-85.

[11]René Spitz, *The Psychoanalytic Study of the Child,* ed. Ruth S. Eissler et al., 25 vols. (New York: International Univs. Press, 1945ff.), 1:53, 2:213.

[12]Akiskal and McKinney, "Depressive Disorders."

[13]John Bowlby, *Attachment* (New York: Basic Books, 1969).

[14]J. Roberston and J. Bowlby, "Responses of Young Children to Separation from Their Mothers," *Courrier Centre Inter Enfance* 2 (1952): 131.

[15]Bowlby, "The Making and Breaking of Affectional Bonds," *Brit. Journ. of Psych.* 130 (1977): 201-10.

[16]J. Birtchnell, "Early Parent Death and Mental Illness," *Brit. Journ. of Psych.* 116 (1970): 281-88; "Recent Parent Death and Mental Illness," ibid., pp. 289-97; "Depression in Relation to Early and Recent Parental Death," ibid., pp. 299-306; id., "Early Parental Death and Psychiatric Diagnosis," *Social Psychiatrist* 7 (1972): 202-10.

[17]L. Camille, "Life Events and Depressive Disorder Reviewed," *Archives* 37 (1980): 529-35.

[18]G. W. Brown, T. Harris and J. R. Copeland, "Depression and Loss," *Brit. Journ. of Psych.* 130 (1977): 1-18.

[19]F. Brown, "Depression and Childhood Bereavement," *Journal of Mental Science* 107 (1961): 754-77.

[20]C. Parkes, "Bereavement and Mental Illness: A Clinical Study of Bereaved Psychiatric Patients," *Brit. Journ. of Psych.* 38 (1965): 1-13; id., "Recent Bereavement As a Cause of Mental Illness," *Brit. Journ. of*

Psych. 110 (1964): 198-204.

[21]A. Schmale, "Relationship of Separation and Depression to Disease," *Psychosomatic Medicine* 20 (1958): 259-77.

[22]E. Bibring, "The Mechanism of Depression," *Affective Disorders*, ed. P. Greenacre (New York: International Univs. Press, 1965), pp. 13-48.

[23]Albert Ellis, "Rational Psychotherapy," *Journal of General Psychology* 59 (1958): 35-49.

[24]A. T. Beck, *Depression: Clinical, Experimental and Theoretical Aspects* (New York: Harper & Row, 1967).

[25]M. Kovacs and A. T. Beck, "Maladaptive Cognitive Structures in Depression," *Amer. Journ. of Psych.* 135 (1978): 5, 525-33; A. J. Rush and A. T. Beck, "Cognitive Therapy of Depression and Suicide," *American Journal of Psychotherapy* 32, No. 2 (1978): 201-19.

[26]A. J. Rush et al., "Comparative Efficacy of Cognitive Therapy and Pharmacotherapy in the Treatment of Depressed Outpatients," *Cognitive Therapy and Research* 1 (1977): 17-37.

[27]Kovacs and Beck, "Maladaptive Cognitive Structures."

[28]E. Becker, *The Revolution in Psychiatry* (London: Free Press of Glencoe, 1964), pp. 108-35.

[29]M. M. Weissman and G. L. Klerman, "Sex Differences and the Epidemiology of Depression," *Archives* 34 (1977): 98-111.

[30]John White, *Eros Defiled* (Downers Grove: InterVarsity Press, 1977), pp. 40-42.

[31]James Olds, "Self-Stimulation and the Brain," *Science* 127 (1958): 315-24.

[32]J. Olds and P. Milner, "Positive Reinforcement Produced by Electrical Stimulation of Septal Area and Other Regions of Rat Brain," *Journal of Comparative Physiology and Psychology* 47 (1954): 419-27.

[33]D. Janowsky et al., "A Cholinergic-Adrenergic Hypothesis of Mania and Depression," *Lancet* 2 (1972): 632-35.

[34]M. Seligman and S. Maier, "Failure to Escape Traumatic Shock," *Journal of Experimental Psychology* 74 (1967): 1-9.

[35]M. Seligman and M. Groves, "Non-Transient Learned Helplessness," *Psychosomatic Science* 19 (1970): 191-92; M. Seligman, *Helplessness: On Depression, Development and Death* (San Francisco: W. H. Freeman & Co., 1975).

[36]V. Riperre, "Comments on Seligman's Theory of Helplessness," *Behavioral Research and Therapy* 15 (1977): 207-09.

[37]M. M. Ter-Pogassion, M. E. Reichle and B. E. Sobel, "Positron-Emission Tomography," *Scientific American*, October 1980, pp. 170-81.

[38]T. A. Wehr, G. Muscettola and F. K. Goodwin, "Urinary 3-Methoxy-4-Hydroxy-Phenylglycol Circadian Rhythm, *Archives* 37 (1980): 257-63; M. Papousek, "Chronobiologische Aspekte der Zyklothymie," *Fortschritte der Neurologischen Psychiatrie* [Progress in neurological psychiatry] 43 (1975): 381-440; T. A. Wehr and F. K. Goodwin, "Biological Rhythms and Affective Illness," *Weekly Psychiatry Update Series* 28

(1978): 1-7; D. F. Kripke et al., "Circadian Rhythm Disorders in Manic-Depressives," *Biological Psychiatry* 13 (1978): 335-44; T. A. Wehr et al., "Phase Advance of the Sleep-Wake Cycle As an Antidepressant," *Science* 206 (1979): 710-13.

Chapter 7

[1] J. J. Schildkraut, "Norepinephrine Metabolites As Biochemical Criteria for Classifying Depressive Disorders and Producing Responses to Treatment: Preliminary Findings," *Amer. Journ. of Psych.* 130 (1973): 695-98.

[2] A. Coopen et al., "Mineral Metabolism in Mania," *Brit. Med. Journ.* 1 (1966): 71-75; C. Perris, "A Study of Bipolar (Manic-Depressive) and Unipolar Recurrent Depressive Psychoses," *Acta Psychiatrica Scandinavica Supplement* 194 (1966): 189.

[3] J. W. Maas, "Biogenic Amines and Depression: Biochemical and Pharmacological Differentiation of Two Types of Depression," *Archives* 32 (1975): 1357-61; M. Astberg et al., "Serotonin Depression—A Biochemical Subgroup within the Affective Disorders?" *Science* 191 (1976): 478-80.

[4] W. E. Bunney, Jr. and M. Davis, "Norepinephrine in Depressive Reactions," *Archives* 13 (1965): 483-94; J. Axelrod, "Biogenicamines and Their Impact on Psychiatry," *Semin Psychiatry* 4 (1972): 199-210; L. L. Iverson, "The Chemistry of the Brain," *Scientific American*, September 1977, p. 134; J. W. Maas, "Biogenic Amines and Depression."

[5] K. Leonhard, *Aufteilung der Endogenen Psychosen* [Division of endogenous psychoses], 1st ed. (Berlin: Akademie-Verlag, 1957); J. W. Chambers and G. M. Brown, "Neurotransmitter of Growth Hormone and A.C.T.H. in Rhesus Monkey: Effects of Biogenic Amines," *Endocrinology* 98 (1976): 420-28; B. J. Carroll, "Studies with Hypothalmic-Pituitary-Adrenal Stimulation Tests in Depression," *Depressive Illness: Some Research Studies*, ed. B. Davis, B. J. Carroll, and R. M. Mobray (Springfield, Ill.: Charles C. Thomas, 1972), pp. 149-201; id., "Psychoendocrine Relationships in Affective Disorders," *Modern Trends in Psychosomatic Medicine*, vol. 3, ed. O. W. Hill (Boston: Butterworths Pub., 1976), pp. 121-53.

[6] L. Traskman et al., "Cortisol in the C.S.F. of Depressed and Suicidal Patients," *Archives* 37 (1980): 761-67.

[7] R. J. Cadoret, "Evidence for Genetic Inheritance of Primary Depressive Disorder in Adoptees," *Amer. Journ. of Psych.* 135, No. 4 (1978): 463-66.

[8] P. S. Applebaum and T. A. Gutheil, "The Boston State Hospital Case: 'Involuntary Mind Control,' the Constitution and the 'Right to Rot,'" *Amer. Journ. of Psych.* 137 (1980): 6.

Chapter 8

[1] Karl Menninger, *Man against Himself* (New York: Harcourt, Brace

& World, 1938), p. 13.

[2] William Cowper and John Newton, *Olney Hymns* (London: T. Nelson and Sons, 1858).

[3] Menninger, pp. 65-66.

[4] P. Sainsbury, "Suicide: Opinions and Facts," *Proceedings of the Royal Society of Medicine* 66 (1973): 579-87.

[5] S. B. Guze and E. Robins, "Suicide and Primary Affective Disorders," *Brit. Journ. of Psych.* 117 (1970): 437-38.

[6] B. Barraclough et al., "A Hundred Cases of Suicide: Clinical Aspects," *Brit. Journ. of Psych.* 125 (1974): 355-73.

[7] Emil Durkheim, *Le Suicide* (1897); trans. *Suicide: A Study in Sociology* (New York: Free Press, 1951).

[8] Ibid., p. 43.

[9] Ibid., p. 44.

[10] Ibid., p. 48.

[11] Ibid., p. 158.

[12] Ibid., p. 208.

[13] Ibid., pp. 208-16.

[14] Ibid., p. 216.

[15] Ibid., p. 241-76.

[16] Ibid., p. 250.

[17] James H. Brown, "Suicide in Britain: More Attempts, Fewer Deaths, Lessons for Public Policy," *Archives* 36 (1974): 1119-24.

[18] Albert Camus, *The Myth of Sisyphus and Other Essays* (New York: Knopf, 1955), p. 3.

[19] C. R. Bagley, "Authoritarianism, Status Integration and Suicide," *Bulletin of Suicidology* 6 (1972): 395-404.

[20] J. H. Brown, "Reporting of Suicides: Canadian Statistics," *Suicide* 5 (1975): 21-28.

[21] D. M. Corey and V. R. Andress, "Alcohol Consumption and Behavior," *Psychological Reports* 40 (1977): 506.

[22] B. Barraclough, "Suicide in the Elderly," *Brit. Journ. of Psych.* Special Publication 6 (1972): 87.

[23] M. I. Solomon and C. P. Hellon, "Suicide and Age in Alberta, Canada, 1951-1977: The Changing Profile," *Archives* 37 (1980): 505-11; id., "Suicide and Age in Alberta, Canada, 1951-1977: A Cohort Analysis," ibid., pp. 510-13; G. E. Murphy and R. D. Wetzel, "Suicide Risk by Birth Cohort in the United States, 1949-1974," ibid., pp. 519-23.

[24] L. I. Dublin and M. Spiegelman, "Longevity and Mortality of American Physicians 1938-1942," *Journal of the American Medical Association* 134 (9 August 1947): 1211; F. G. Dickinson and L. W. Martin, "Physician Mortality 1949-1951," *Journal of the AMA* 162 (1956): 1462; P. H. Blachly, H. T. Osterud and R. Josslin, "Suicide in Professional Groups," *New England Journal of Medicine* 268 (6 June 1963): 1278; P. H. Blachly, W. Disher and G. Roduner, "Suicide by Physicians," *Bulletin of Suicidology* 4 (December 1968): 1; A. G. Craig and F. J. Pitts, Jr., "Suicide by

Physicians," *Diseases of the Nervous System* 29 (1968): 763; K. D. Rose and I. Rosow, "Physicians Who Kill Themselves," *Archives* 29 (1973): 800.

[25]P. H. Blachly et al., "Suicide by Physicians," pp. 1-18.

[26]W. Freeman, "Psychiatrists Who Kill Themselves: A Study of Suicide," *Amer. Journ. of Psych.* 126 (1967): 846-47.

[27]Ibid.

[28]R. Eastwood, *Preventive Medicine and Public Health,* ed. J. Last (New York: Appleton-Century-Crofts, 1980).

[29]"Editorial: Suicide among Doctors," *Brit. Med. Journ.* 1 (1964): 789-90.

[30]W. A. Kelly, "Suicide and Psychiatric Education," *Amer. Journ. of Psych.* 130, No. 4 (1973): 463-67.

[31]E. S. Paykel, "Classification of Depressed Patients: A Cluster Analysis Derived Grouping," *Brit. Journ. of Psych.* 118 (1971): 275-88.

[32]M. M. Weissman, K. Fox and G. L. Klerman, "Hostility and Depression Associated with Suicide Attempts," *Amer. Journ. of Psych.* 130, No. 4 (1973): 450-55.

[33]Menninger, p. 64.

[34]A. T. Beck, "Thinking and Depression," *Archives* 9 (1963): 324-33; K. Minkoff et al., "Hopelessness, Depression and Attempted Suicide," *Amer. Journ. of Psych.* 130, No. 4 (1973): 445-59.

[35]E. S. Schneidman, "Suicide," *Comprehensive Textbook of Psychiatry,* ed. A. M. Freedman, H. I. Kaplan and B. J. Sadock (Baltimore: Williams & Wilkins Co., 1975), pp. 1774-85.

[36]Menninger, p. 14.

Chapter 9

[1]H. L. P. Reznik et al., "Videotape Confrontation after Suicide Attempt," *Amer. Journ. of Psych.* 130, No. 4 (1973): 460-63.

[2]C. R. Bagley, "The Evaluation of a Suicide Prevention Scheme by an Ecological Method," *Social Science and Medicine* 2 (1976): 1-14.

[3]B. M. Barraclough, C. Jennings and J. R. Moss, "Suicide Prevention by the Samaritans: A Controlled Study of Effectiveness," *Lancet* 2 (1977): 237-39.

[4]Bagley.

[5]J. H. Brown, "Suicide in Britain."

[6]N. Kreitman, "The Coal Gas Story: The United Kingdom Suicide Rates, 1960-71," *British Journal of Preventive Social Medicine* 30 (1976): 86-93.

Chapter 10

[1]D. Martyn Lloyd-Jones, *Spiritual Depression: Its Causes & Cure* (Grand Rapids, Mich.: Eerdmans, 1965), p. 18.

[2]S. Arieti, "A Psychotherapeutic Approach to Severely Depressed Patients," *Amer. Journ. of Psychotherapy* 32, No. 1 (1978): 33-47.

[3]Nathan A. Kline, *From Sad to Glad* (New York: Ballantine Books, 1975).

[4]L. Luborsky, J. Mintz and A. Averbach, "Predicting the Outcome of Psychotherapy," *Archives* 37 (1980): 471-81.

[5]P. Clayton, J. Halikas and W. Maurice, "The Depression of Widowhood," *Brit. Journ. of Psych.* 120 (1972): 71-77.

[6]F. Brown, "Depression and Childhood Bereavement," *Journal of Mental Science* 107 (1961): 754-77; H. F. Harlow, "The Nature of Love," *American Psychologist* 13 (1958): 673-85.

[7]B. A. Prosoff et al., "Research Diagnostic Criteria Sub-Types of Depression: Their Role As Predictors of Differential Response to Psychotherapy and Drug Treatment," *Archives* 37 (1980): 796-801.

[8]George Kelly, *The Psychology of Personal Constructs* (New York: W. W. Norton & Co., 1955).

[9]Albert Ellis, *The Essence of Rational Psychotherapy: A Comprehensive Approach to Treatment* (New York: Institute for Rational Living, 1971).

[10]Aaron T. Beck, *Cognitive Therapy and Emotional Disorders* (New York: International Univs. Press, 1979).

[11]Rush and Beck, *Cognitive Therapy of Depression and Suicide."*

[12]Jerome Yesavage, "A Kantian Critique of Cognitive Psychotherapy," *Amer. Journ. of Psychotherapy* 1 (1980): 99-105.

[13]Ibid.

[14]A. Ellis, "A Consideration of Some of the Objections to Rational Emotive Psychotherapy," *Reason and Emotion in Psychotherapy,* ed. Lyle Stuart (Secaucus, N. J.: Citadel Press, 1977), pp. 331-74.

[15]R. P. Liberman and D. E. Raskins, "Depression: A Behavioural Formulation," *Archives* 24 (1971): 515-23.

[16]A. A. Lazarus, "Learning Theory and the Treatment of Depression," *Behavioral Research and Therapy* 6 (1968): 83-89.

[17]T. Kora, "Korita Therapy," *International Journal of Psychiatry* 1 (1965): 611-40.

[18]Frank Lake, *Clinical Theology* (London: Darton, Longman and Todd, 1973), pp. 103-04.

Chapter 11

[1]R. A. Brathwaite, R. T. Goulding et al., "Plasma Concentration of Amitriptyline and Clinical Response," *Lancet* (June 1972): 1297-1300; A. H. Glassman et al., "Clinical Implications of Imipramine Plasma Levels for Depressive Illness," *Archives* 34 (1977): 197-204; L. F. Gram et al., "Plasma Levels and Antidepressant Effects of Imipramine," *Clinical Pharmacological Therapeutics* 19 (1976): 318-24; N. Reisby et al., "Imipramine: Clinical Effects and Pharmacokinetic Variability," *Psychopharmacology* 54 (1977): 263-72.

[2]D. Luchins and J. Ananth, "Therapeutic Implications of Tricyclic Antidepressant Plasma Levels," *Journal of Nervous and Mental Diseases* 162 (1976): 430-36.

[3]J. Mendels and J. Giacomo, "The Treatment of Depression with a Single Daily Dose of Imipramine Parmoate," *Amer. Journ. of Psych.* 130 (1973): 1022-24; C. E. Schorer, "Single Dose versus Divided Dose of Imipramine," *Psychopharmacology* 28 (1973): 115-19; C. C. Weise et al., "Amitrip-

tyline Once Daily versus Three Times Daily in Depressed Outpatients,"
Archives 37 (1980): 555-60.

[4]D. C. Moir et al., "Cardiotoxicity of Tricyclic Antidepressants," *Proceedings of the British Pharmacological Society* 4 (1972): 371-72.

[5]D. F. Klein and J. M. Davis, *Diagnosis and Drug Treatment of Psychiatric Disorders* (Baltimore: Williams & Wilkins Co., 1969).

[6]M. R. Liebowitz et al., American Psychiatric Association, 1979.

[7]A. Reifman and R. J. Wyatt, "Lithium: A Break in the Rising Cost of Mental Illness," *Archives* 37 (1980): 385-88.

[8]B. Reisberg and S. Gershon, "Side Effects Associated with Lithium Therapy," *Archives* 36 (1979): 879-87; F. A. Jenner, "Lithium and the Question of Kidney Damage," *Archives* 36 (1979): 888-90; P. Ciraf et. al., "Patient Selection for Long-Term Lithium Treatment in Clinical Practice," *Archives* 36 (1979): 894-97.

[9]P. C. Baastrup et al., "Prophylactic Lithium: Double-Blind Discontinuation in Manic-Depressive and Recurrent Depressive Disorders," *Lancet* 1 (1970): 326-30; A. Coppen et al., "Prophylactic Lithium in Affective Disorders," *Lancet* 2 (1979): 275-79; R. I. Cundall, P. W. Brooks and L. G. Murray, "Controlled Evaluation of Lithium Prophylaxis in Affective Disorders," *Psychological Medicine* 3 (1972): 308-11; R. R. Fieve, T. Kumbarachi and D. L. Dunner, "Lithium Prophylaxis of Depression in Bipolar I, Bipolar II and Unipolar Patients," *Amer. Journ. of Psych.* 133 (1976): 925-29; R. P. Hullin, R. McDonald and M. N. Allsopp, "Prophylactic Lithium in Recurrent Affective Disorders," *Lancet* 1 (1972): 1044-46; R. F. Prien, E. M. Caffey and C. J. Klett, "Prophylactic Efficacy of Lithium Carbonate in Manic-Depressive Illness: Report of the Veterans Administration and National Institute of Mental Health Collaborative Study Group," *Archives* 28 (1973): 337-41; id., "Lithium Carbonate and Imipramine in Prevention of Affective Episodes: A Comparison in Recurrent Affective Illness," *Archives* 29 (1973): 420-25; F. Quitkin et al., "The Prophylactic Effect of Lithium and Imipramine in Bipolar II and Unipolar Patients: A Preliminary Report," *Amer. Journ. of Psych.* 135 (1978): 570-72.

[10]C. P. L. Freeman, "Electroconvulsive Therapy: Its Current Clinical Use," *British Journal of Hospital Medicine* (March 1979): 281-92.

[11]Medical Research Council, "Clinical Trial of the Treatment of Depressive Illness," *Brit. Med. Journ.* 1 (1965): 881-86; O. Bratfos and J. O. Haug, "Electroconvulsive Therapy and Antidepressant Drugs in Manic-Depressive Disease, Treatment Results at Discharge and Three Months Later," *Acta Psychiatrica Scandinavica* 41 (1965): 588-96; M. Greenblatt, G. H. Grosser and H. Wechsler, "Differential Response of Hospitalized Depressed Patients to Somatic Therapy," *Amer. Journ. of Psych.* 120 (1964): 935-43; A Hordern, C. G. Burt and H. F. Holt, *Depressive States: A Pharmacotherapeutic Study* (Springfield, Ill.: Charles C. Thomas, 1965); J. Angst, E. Varga and M. Shepherd, "Preliminary Report of a Retrospective Study of the Treatments of Depression," *Proceedings of the Fifth International*

Congress of the Collegium Internationale Neuropsychopharmacologicum (Washington, D.C., 1966), pp. 536-38; D. H. Avery and G. Winokur, "The Efficacy of Electroconvulsive Therapy and Antidepressants in Depression," *Biological Psychiatry* 12 (1977): 507-23.

[12] J. Hughes, B. M. Barraclough and W. Reeve, "Are Patients Shocked by ECT?" *Journ. of the Royal Society of Medicine* 74 (1981): 283-85.

[13] J. L. Barton, "ECT in Depression: The Evidence of Controlled Studies," *Biological Psychiatry* 12, No. 5 (1974): 687-97.

[14] D. G. Grahame-Smith, A. R. Green and D. W. Costain, "Mechanism of Antidepressant Action of Electroconvulsive Therapy," *Lancet* 1 (1978): 254-75.

[15] L. R. Squire and P. Slater, "Bilateral and Unilateral ECT: Effects on Verbal and Non-Verbal Memory," *Amer. Journ. of Psych.* 135, No. 11 (1978): 1316-20.

[16] L. R. Squire and P. M. Chase, "Memory Function 6-9 Months after Electroconvulsive Therapy," *Archives* 32 (1975): 1557-64.

[17] G. D'Elia and H. Raotoma, "Is Unilateral ECT Less Effective Than Bilateral ECT?" *Brit. Journ. of Psych.* 126 (1975): 83-89.

[18] D. Avery and A. Lubrano, "Depression Treated with Imipramine and ECT: The De Carolis Study Reconsidered," *Amer. Journ. of Psych.* 136, No. 4B (1979): 559-62.

[19] I. C. Wilson et al., "A Controlled Study of Treatments of Depression," *Journal of Neuropsychiatry* 4 (1963): 331-37.

[20] *American Psychiatric Association Task Force on Electroconvulsive Therapy*, September 1978, p. 82.

[21] D. Avery and G. Winokur, "Mortality in Depressed Patients with Electroconvulsive Therapy and Antidepressants," *Archives* 33 (1976): 1029-37.

[22] Avery and Winokur, "Suicide, Attempted Suicide, and Relapsed Rates in Depression," *Archives* 35 (1978): 749-53.

[23] D. Wasylenki, "Depression in the Elderly," *Canadian Medical Association Journal* 122 (1980): 525-40; J. O. Cavenar, A. A. Maltbie and L. Austin, "Depression Simulating Organic Brain Disease," *Amer. Journ. of Psych.* 136, No. 4B (1979): 521-23.

[24] "The Experience of Electroconvulsive Therapy," *Brit. Journ. of Psych.* 3 (1965): 365-67.

Index

Read on for further titles in the

JOHN WHITE LIBRARY

Eros Defiled
JOHN WHITE

To be human is to be sexual. That's the way God made us.

Yet many people – Christians included – are tormented by their sexuality. The problem may be frustration, masturbation, premarital sex and perhaps pregnancy, an 'affair', homosexuality, or strange compulsions.

To those people and their counsellors, John White offers compassion, help and hope.

'. . . a refreshing direct book. It . . . shows a great deal of sensitivity, and has no fear of straight speaking.'   *Christian Weekly Newspapers*

'The book's arguments are carefully anchored in the Bible. Undoubtedly *Eros Defiled* should be required reading for all in the pastoral ministry . . . Youth leaders . . . parents too. It can be recommended also to Christian adolescents in their late teens.'

Evangelical Times

168 pages   Pocketbook

Inter-Varsity Press

The Cost of Commitment
JOHN WHITE

'For years I felt guilty because I never seemed to be committed deeply enough to Christ . . . I had the feeling that I should be suffering more, doing without more. Yet when I did suffer, my suffering bore little relationship to my commitment. Sometimes it seemed to arise from my lack of commitment and at other times bore no relation at all to it . . .

'When Jesus tells you to take up your cross daily, he is not telling you to find some way to suffering daily. He is simply giving forewarning of what happens to the person who follows him.'

A warm and personal book to help Christians count the cost of commitment.

'. . . message is presented in a lucid, readable, at times very moving style . . .'   *Evangelical Times*

'. . . useful book to place into the hands of those who have recently made the great decision.'   *Christian Herald*

92 pages   Pocketbook

Inter-Varsity Press

The Fight
JOHN WHITE

John White has written this book because he wants you to understand clearly what the Christian life is all about. He wants you to learn in the depths of your being that the eternal God loves you and plans only your highest good – more trust in him, more likeness to him.

But his love will bring pain as intense as your joy. For the Christian life is a fight . . .

'Reading *The Fight* is to inhale great draughts of fresh air into one's Christian life . . . This is the kind of book every 20th Century Christian should have on his book shelf.'   *Christian Weekly Newspapers*

230 pages   Pocketbook

Inter-Varsity Press

Parents in Pain
JOHN WHITE

Are you a parent?
How will you react if your child gets involved in drugs, crime, sleeping around, alcoholism? Will you blame yourself? your child? society?

Whether you are a parent, potential parent, or friend, this book will help you. It describes what you can do and what you can't. Recognising the limits of your responsibility will save you from needless anguish and self-blame. This is a book to help you meet difficulties with courage and confidence.

'. . . offers the kind of help no Christian parent can afford to miss.'
Family (formerly *Life of Faith*)

'This is an important book . . .'   *Renewal*

242 pages   Pocketbook

Inter-Varsity Press

People in Prayer
JOHN WHITE

Ten portraits of people in prayer to God.

People pleading, praising, confessing, interceding. People being changed as they draw closer to God.

God – wanting communication with human beings. With you.

'Go after this book – get it and read it! It will challenge and disturb but you will not regret it.' *Grace Magazine*

'. . . the contents proved so helpful. At all times practical, open, and in touch with our own times.' *Reaper* (New Zealand)

'This is a wholesome book, penetrating in its insight and profound in its encouragements.' *Life and Work*

'It is impossible to read this book without being driven to the Master's feet, with one simple petition, "Lord, teach us to pray".' *Christian Herald*

160 pages   Pocketbook

Inter-Varsity Press

The Race
The Christian way in faith and practice
JOHN WHITE

Twenty-eight magazine-style articles and modern parables from the pen of one of Christendom's most lucid and exciting authors.

The topics range from the virgin birth and the inspiration of the Bible to depression and the problem of pain. Parables (try 'The orange trees' or 'The parrot fish'!) make the truth both compelling and entertaining.

The Race is a many-faceted gem of a book.

'Splendid, pithy teaching.' *Christian Weekly Newspapers*

226 pages   Pocketbook

Inter-Varsity Press